KERSTIN BRÄTSCH

ΔΕΣΤΕ

DESTE Foundation for Contemporary Art

KERSTIN BRÄTSCH

2000 WORDS

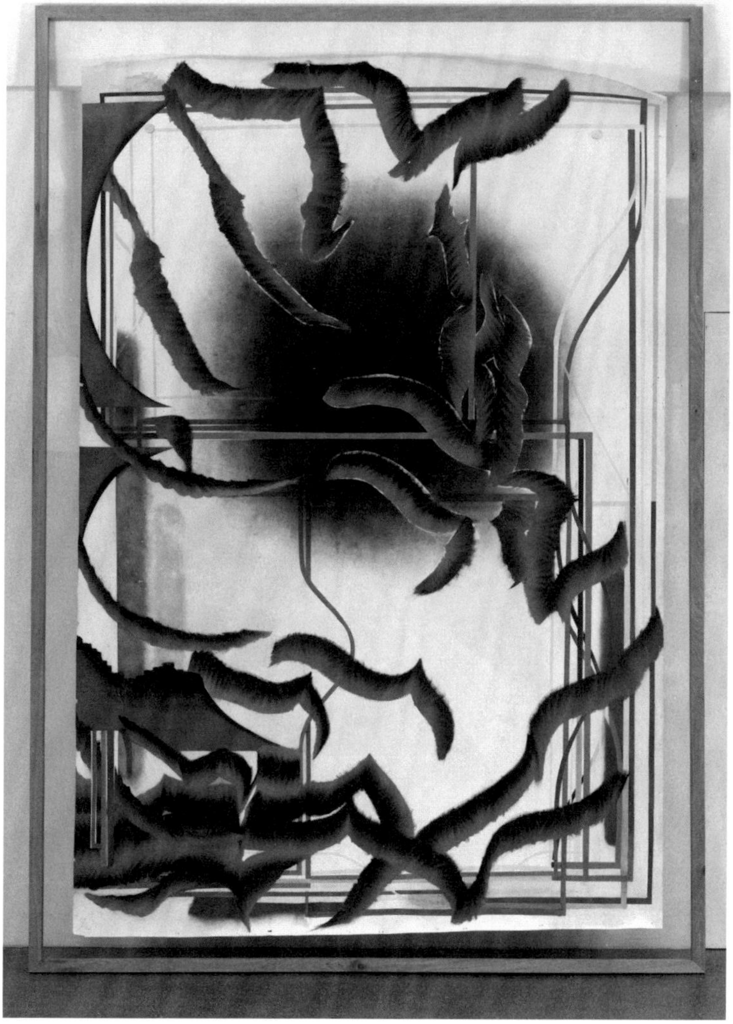

NOTES ON ABSTRACTION

Massimiliano Gioni

For Kerstin Brätsch, painting is a tile in a mosaic of languages that range from drawing to performance, from sculpture to design, by way of theater and fashion. Painting is also a link in a system of production, distribution, and transformation—a constant exercise in lateral shifts, through which a painting can become a book, a sculpture, the set for a performance, or, more mysteriously, turn into a phantom image of itself.

The artist's identity seems to follow a similar path, moving freely from the personal to the collective. Brätsch, in fact, inhabits the paradox of using painting to delocalize subjectivity. Historically, painting—and more specifically the brushstroke, which is one of Brätsch's most frequently recurring motifs—is assumed to voice individual expression. In Brätsch's work, subjectivity instead proliferates into an endless digression of alter egos and imaginary corporations, from Kerstin Brätsch to DAS INSTITUT, KAYA, and UNITED BROTHERS, to name just a few of the collaborations and fictional firms she has initiated or participated in.

The voices of multiple traditions of twentieth-century abstract painting echo and resonate in Brätsch's work, as she digests entire stylistic vocabularies with ease, processing them into a unique composite. But there is no referentialism or historical obsession in her work. On the contrary, there is a pride in seeming absolutely contemporary and of the moment, with the awareness, however, that the era we live in is also based on the synchronicity and permeability of languages, as if every style were always on hand, within reach, but never completely assimilable.

Painting in the age of Wikipedia: information overload—maximum elasticity, minimum absorption. Painting as surface tension. Total accessibility and permanent distance—history as assemblage.

Among the artists whose traces and legacies are to be found in Brätsch's work, one could list Hilma af Klint, René Daniëls, Sonia Delaunay, Emma Kunz, František Kupka, Bridget Riley, and Rudolf Steiner. Encrusted here too are much more prosaic visual languages: old advertisements, worn photocopies, decorative motifs, computer graphics, patterns from cheap fabric, photographs from mail-order catalogs. Perhaps there is also the hidden influence of Franz West's *Passstücke* (Adaptives)—sculptures that can be used as strange theatrical props—and a return to the experimental fluidity of the 1960s, in the footsteps of Robert Rauschenberg and his ability to move freely between painting, dance, and choreography.

One wonders if Brätsch is interested less in abstraction than in forms of obstruction, concealment, and dissimulation. She seems stubbornly determined not to be *just* a painter, although painting is her vocation. In all of her work, one senses an effort to escape from the narrow confines of painting, to create instead a form of art that cannot be immediately traced to a single genre. Between diverging impulses and attitudes, Brätsch's painting strikes a precarious balance—an "abstract anxiety," as the artist calls it.

Many of Brätsch's works have an irresolute way of occupying space: they are hung from magnets, stretched out like bedsheets in the wind, suspended on wooden frames, or left on the ground like clothes torn off in the heat of an amorous encounter. Brätsch's painting is environmental and spatial, but often takes a marginal position within the exhibition space, off to the side, as if somewhat insecure. Her painting is first and foremost an attitude, not a style. In Brätsch's work, forms become attitudes.

Brätsch's objects and artworks often trigger actions or generate other products, as in a chain reaction. The artist updates action painting to the digital age: this is information painting, or painting as transmission. The canvas is not an arena, but a screen overlaid with multiple windows and enlarged pixels—an info dump.

In the age of the screen, according to critic John Kelsey, artists are "producing images of communication," turning painting into "a picture of information without a message."[1] Art historian David Joselit has compared contemporary painting—particularly the various forms of abstraction today—to "a broadcast medium." Joselit writes that painting today is "nothing but transmission—as well as, simultaneously, the transmission of nothing."[2] Many artists of Brätsch's generation "use painting to narrate, or to demonstrate phenomenologically ... the social life of images."[3] Painting thus serves as "a model of how information travels and a method for measuring the distance—geographic, temporal, social, and psychic—between enunciations of the same picture."[4]

This type of information painting—this "corporate abstraction," as Brätsch has called it—offers the most fitting visual analogy for a form of advanced capitalism that has become progressively more abstract and volatile, immaterial and ungraspable in its vastness. As the means of production and means of communication become perfectly aligned, as packaging becomes content, Kelsey warns against such confluences. "The more effective strategies," he writes, "will from now on involve using flatness, abstraction, and reproduction against themselves, and convert these into forces of heterogeneity instead."[5]

In its centrifugal movement outside the limits of painting, Brätsch's work is connected to an entire tradition of applied arts and industrial design. Especially in the series of works created under the pseudonym DAS INSTITUT—a fictional "import/export agency" established by Brätsch and Adele Röder—one can feel the echo of the Bauhaus and, even before that, of the arts and crafts movement. But these referents are somehow corroded by a new sense of urgency and immediacy, debased by a certain cheapness that is very much of our present time. DAS INSTITUT is Bauhaus by way of the sweatshops of the Far East. DAS INSTITUT is Bauhaus meets disco design.

Craftsmanship—or the destruction thereof—is of paramount importance to Brätsch's project. After half a decade spent expanding the field of painting from within, in recent years Brätsch has embarked on a series of experiments in which she has taught herself techniques that historically belong to the applied arts. From her glass paintings to her recent marblings, Brätsch has been collaborating with various artisans to bend decorative practices to new ends, in a productive contamination of traditions, both high and low, that scrambles technical skills into unconventional methodologies. For example, in her *Unstable Talismanic Renderings* (2014–17, p. 68–69; realized in collaboration with master marbler Dirk Lange), marbling paper—a technique mainly used in book binding to decorate endpapers, and typically considered a "minor" art form—is pushed to a new scale. This series of large paintings on paper takes the cosmic iconography of abstract expressionism and color-field painting—with the attendant mythology of chance operations and heroic gestures—and forces it to unexpected conclusions. With their amoebic explosions of colors, these works summon a sense of spiritual depth achieved with the most prosaic of means. A combination of the celestial and the quotidian is caught in a short circuit of sorts.

Not dissimilar is the process through which Brätsch has realized her paintings and sculptures in glass, for which she has worked with the stained-glass painter Urs Rickenbach, who collaborated with artist Sigmar Polke on his last Gesamtkunstwerk, the decorations of the windows of the Grossmünster church in Zurich. In her glass works Brätsch simultaneously undermines and glorifies the legacy of her predecessors and teachers, engaging once more in a cross-wiring of the minor and the major, which erases traditional distinctions and established hierarchies. In these works, then, Brätsch performs the roles of both artist and artisan, teacher and apprentice, while at the same time aiming at taking the *man* out of *craftsmanship*, by playing with historical narratives typically associated with male figures and masters.

In Brätsch's system, every role can be swapped and every object is interchangeable, just as the borders between painting, design, and sculpture have become porous. For some paintings, Brätsch and DAS INSTITUT have come up with a series of posters and commercials to promote the works as if they were commodities. And paintings themselves have been printed onto scarves and shawls to be worn as clothing. On other occasions, Brätsch has displayed paintings as carpets, suspending them above neon lights, or unrolled them on tanning beds and scanners, in what could be described as a radical reinterpretation of the "flatbed picture plane," which art historian Leo Steinberg identified as one of Rauschenberg's greatest contributions to the history of painting. Brätsch updates the vocabulary of abstraction by mixing it with a vernacular of technical information and commercial expertise.

Abstraction as a vehicle toward the absolute is one of the most burdensome legacies of the twentieth century. Brätsch seems to be searching for new ways to confront this tradition, striving for the sublime without falling into the snares of kitsch. Throughout her practice, references to spirituality abound—from the *Psychics* series (2007–8) to the *Unstable Talismanic Renderings*, via her work in glass—but they are hacked, ventriloquized, as though the legacy of certain histories were to be both celebrated and debunked.

Strange, vaguely larval forms loom out of

the large drawings that compose Brätsch's *Psychics* series; here and there, one can glimpse the oval of a face, the shape of a head. The paintings in this series are not aura portraits or the projections of some kind of obscure force. Rather, they open a pictorial space in which the absolutist urges of early twentieth-century abstract painting coexist with much lighter, more contemporary forms of notation. Elsewhere, one finds large, wide-open, oddly animal-like eyes, and swarms of protocellular life whose planes of color ripple like television static. The faces that sometimes float up to the surface have the gaseous substance of a revelation. These are contemporary icons—icons as both religious paintings and computer graphics: a digital sublime.

Many of Brätsch's paintings live a double life. They exist as themselves and as shadows of their former beings. Painted on sheets of Mylar and plastic, these works—which Brätsch informally calls "ghosts" (2009)—adopt the same motifs, shapes, and colors used in her works on paper but repeat them on transparent backgrounds. This repetition and dematerialization is a process that demystifies and critiques Brätsch's work from the inside. It is as if these transparent copies strip the artist's previous paintings of all weight, rendering them more volatile. Brätsch's phantom copies are not faithful reproductions, but variations on a theme. Actually, one could say that all of Brätsch's work rests on the very negation of any difference between original and copy: all of her paintings are originals and all are copies. Some of Brätsch's abstractions are reproductions of computer-generated graphic motifs that actually derive from patterns digitally drawn by her collaborators, which she diligently enlarges and reproduces on paper. Through these repetitions and endless translations across media, Brätsch—like many artists of her generation—elevates painting as if to compete with the industry of the digital imaginary and its distribution.

As refracted in these and other works, Brätsch's paintings appear to inhabit multiple lives and multiple states of being. Perhaps her goal is to no longer be considered a painter, to finally be seen as the owner of a conceptual import/export agency, a trader in the market of pure information, an aesthete of communication, a hacker of forms, a data mystic.

1 John Kelsey, "100%," in *Rich Texts: Selected Writing for Art* (Berlin: Sternberg Press, 2010), 17, 21.

2 David Joselit, "Signal Processing: Abstraction Then and Now," *Artforum* 49, no. 10 (Summer 2011): 360.

3 Ibid, 361.

4 Ibid.

5 John Kelsey, "Decapitalism," in *Rich Texts*, 73.

WORKS

DAS INSTITUT
THUS! Unit 4, 2010

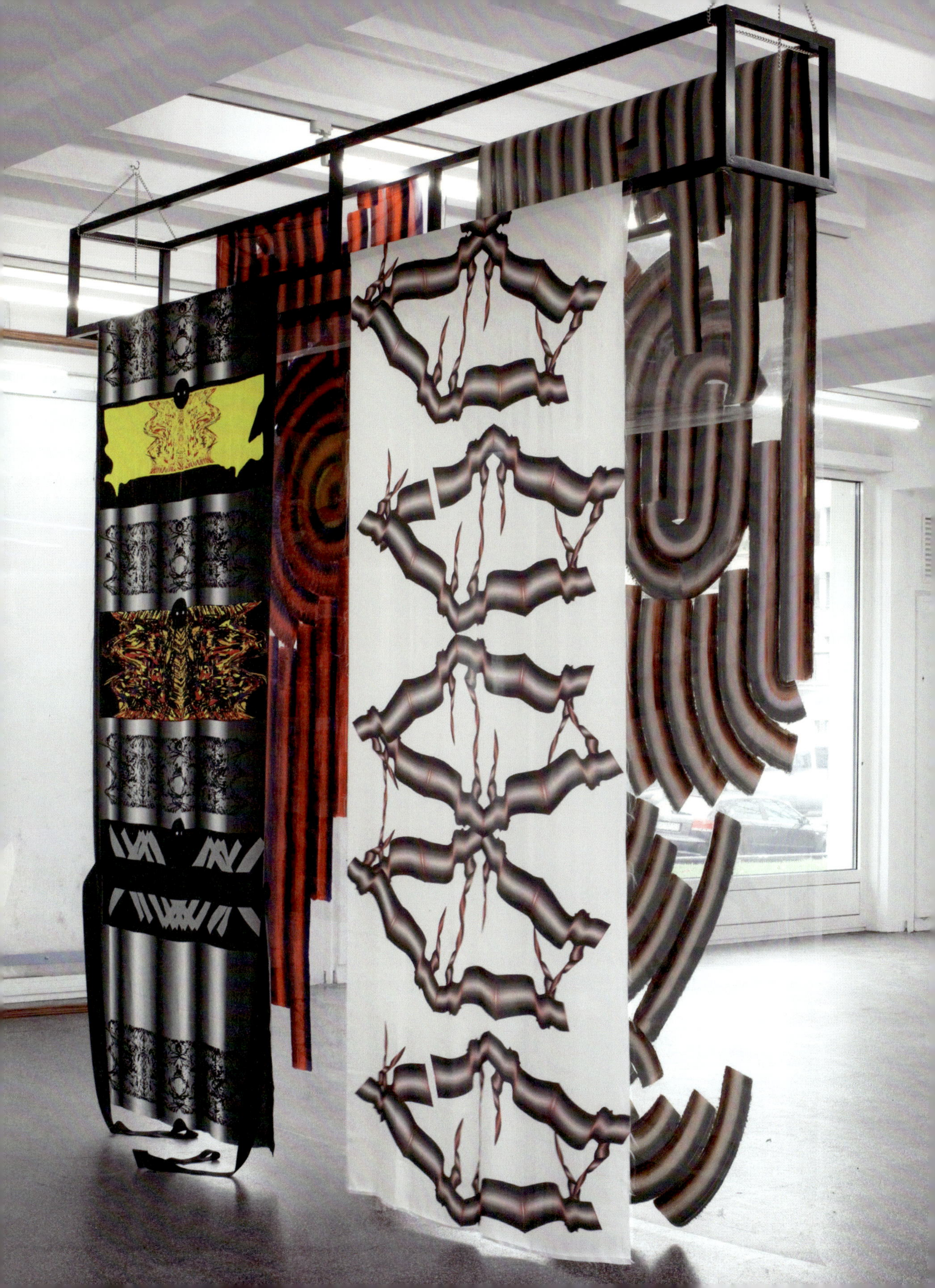

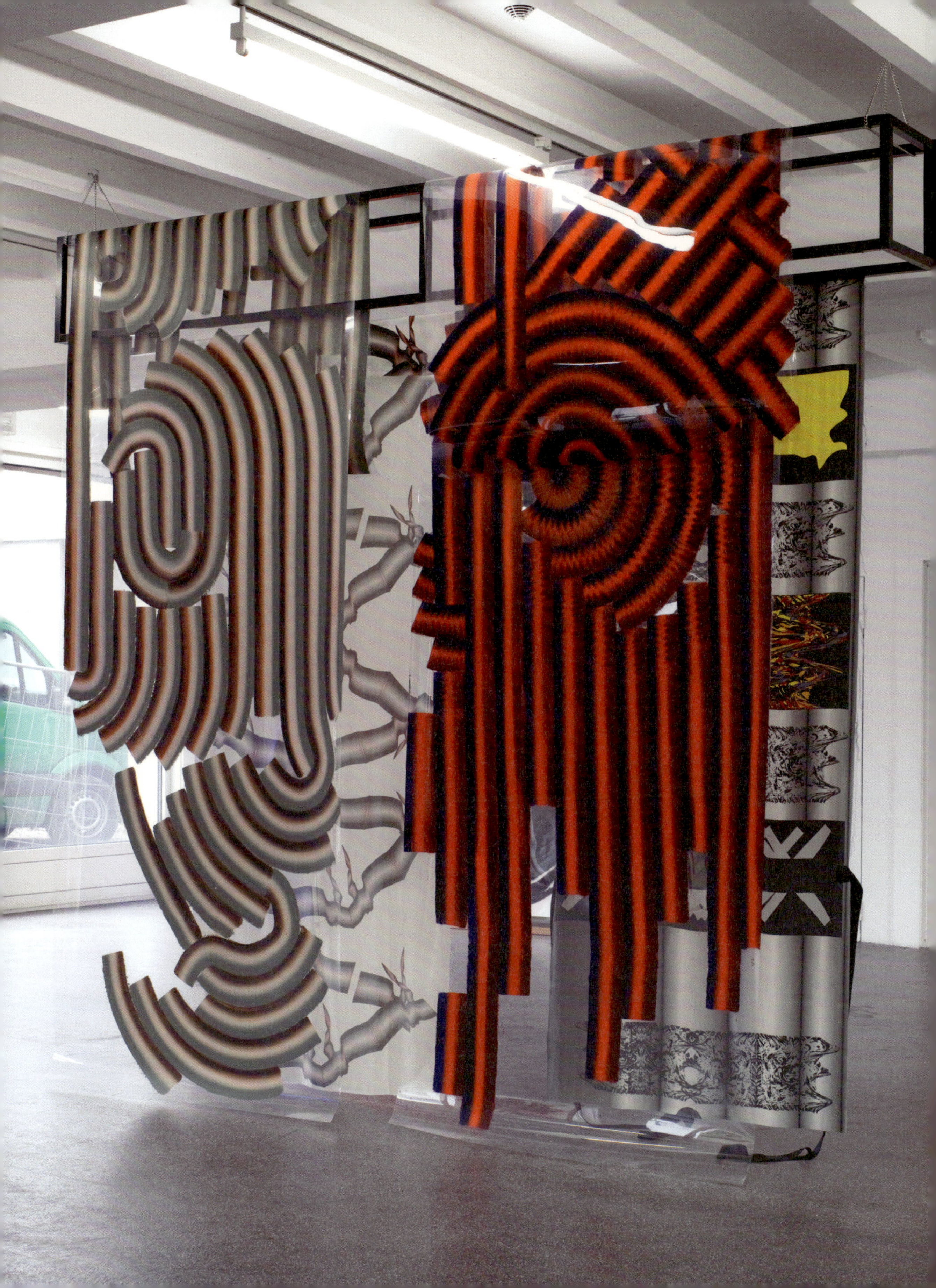

Kerstin Brätsch for DAS INSTITUT
But Your Soul Is Too Big It Would Stick Out Everywhere, 2011
(from the series Corporate Abstraction)

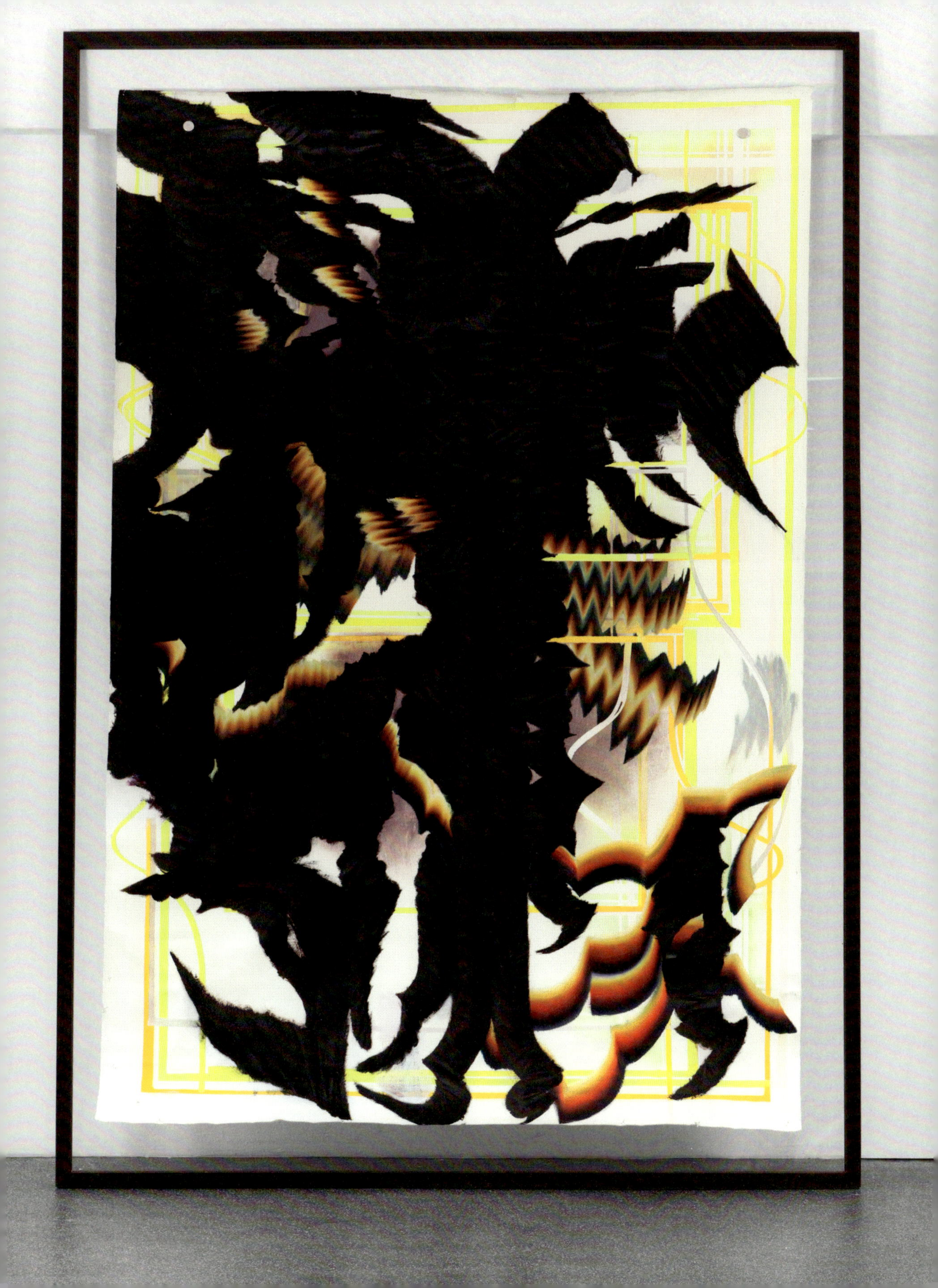

Kerstin Brätsch for DAS INSTITUT
Luxus, Askese, Cocoonin, Neo Neo Biedermeier, 2011

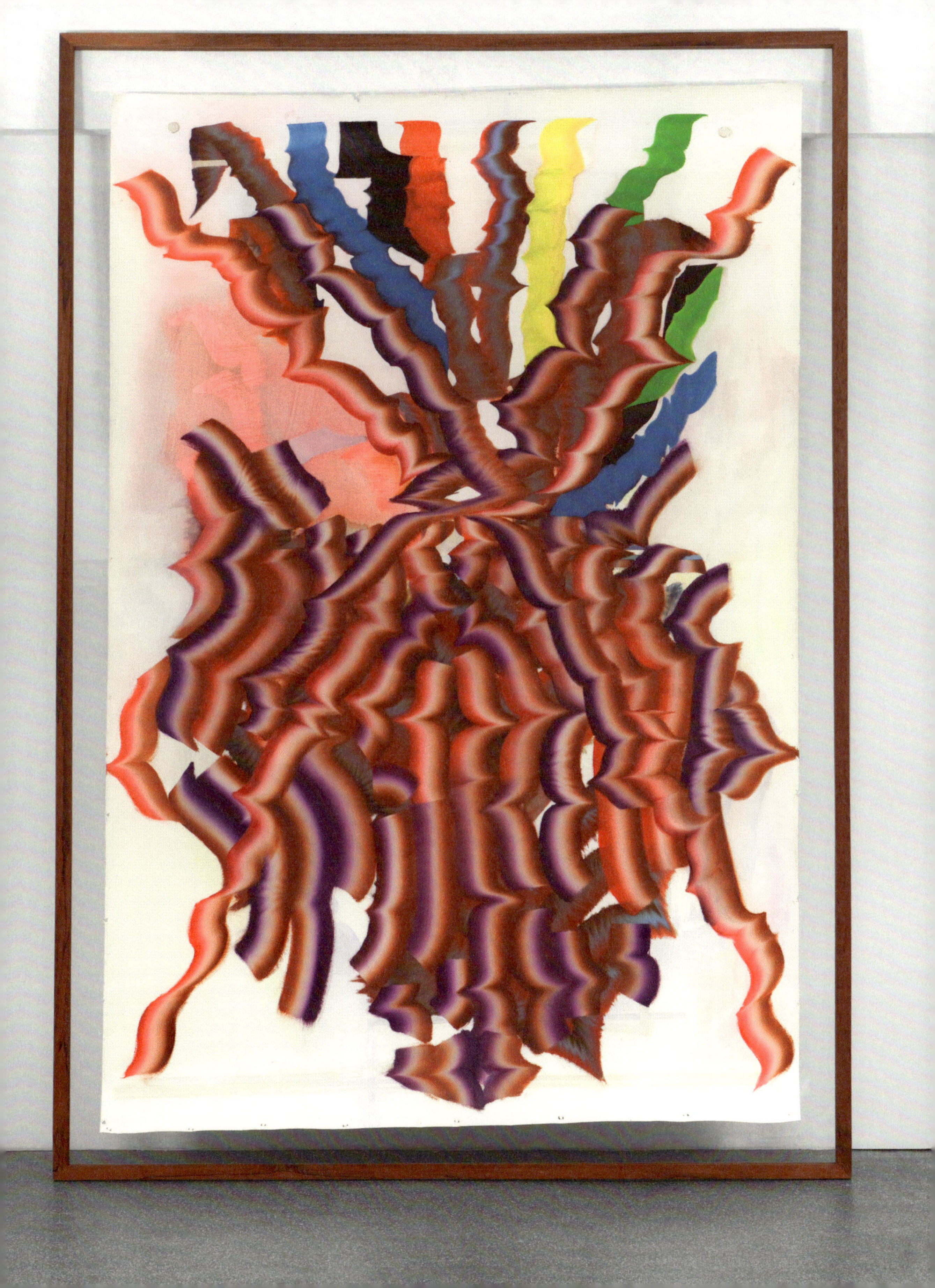

Kerstin Brätsch for DAS INSTITUT
The Random / The Violent Effect, 2011

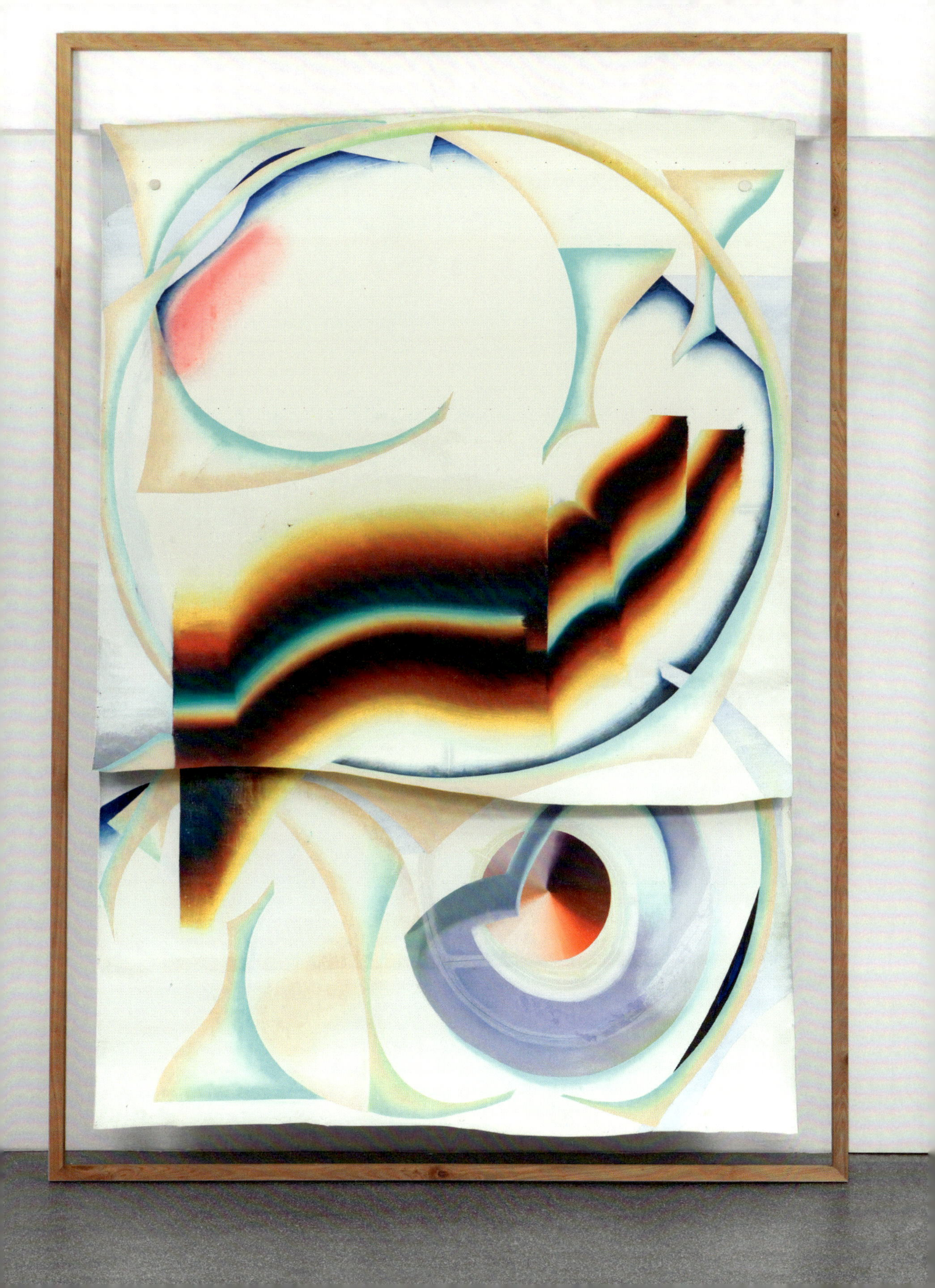

Kerstin Brätsch for DAS INSTITUT
Also Known As, 2011 (from the series Corporate Abstraction)

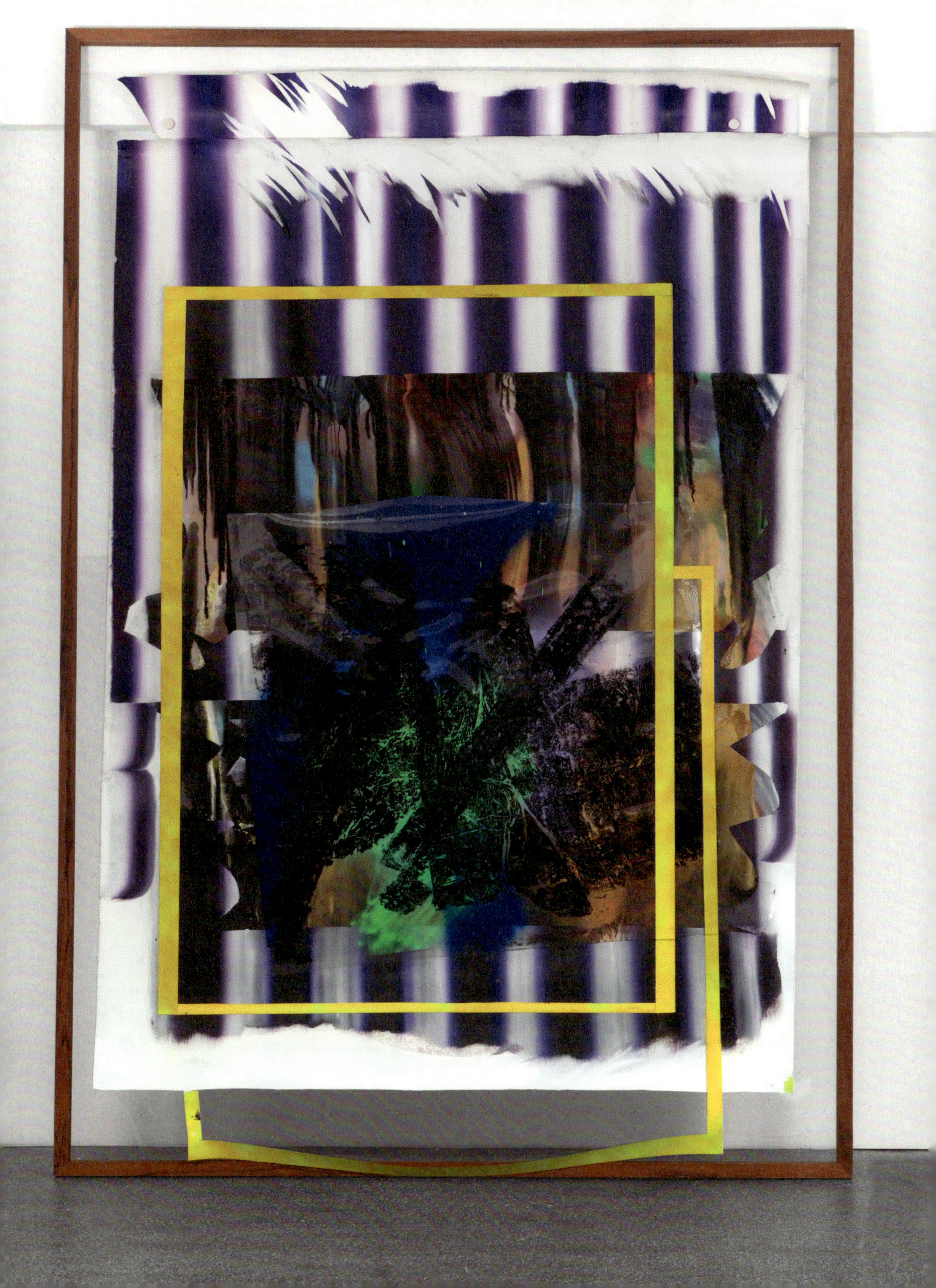

Kerstin Brätsch for DAS INSTITUT
Main Street Left, Second Right, 2011 (from the series Corporate Abstraction)

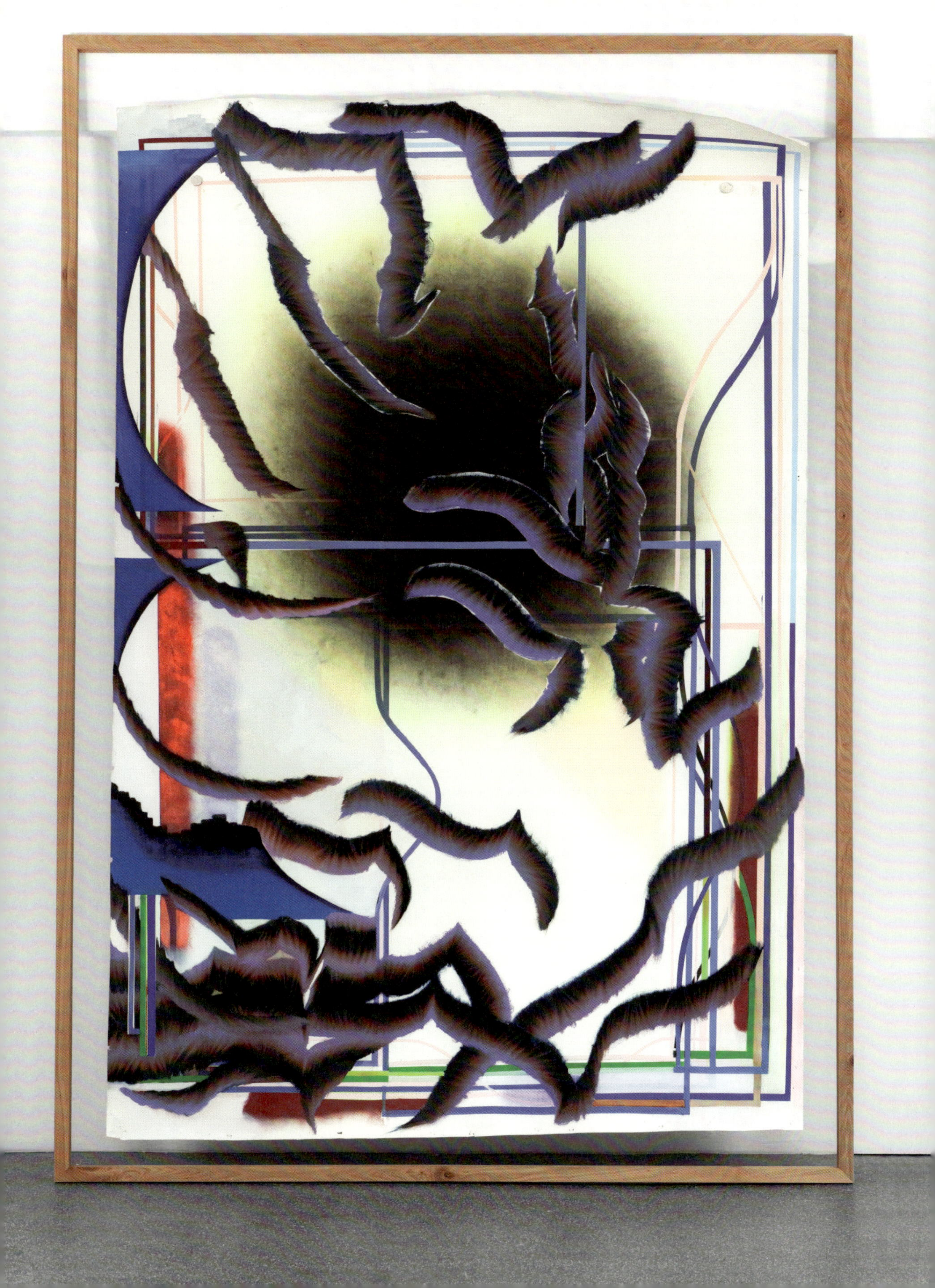

Kerstin Brätsch for DAS INSTITUT
This Is Not It, 2011 (from the series Corporate Abstraction)

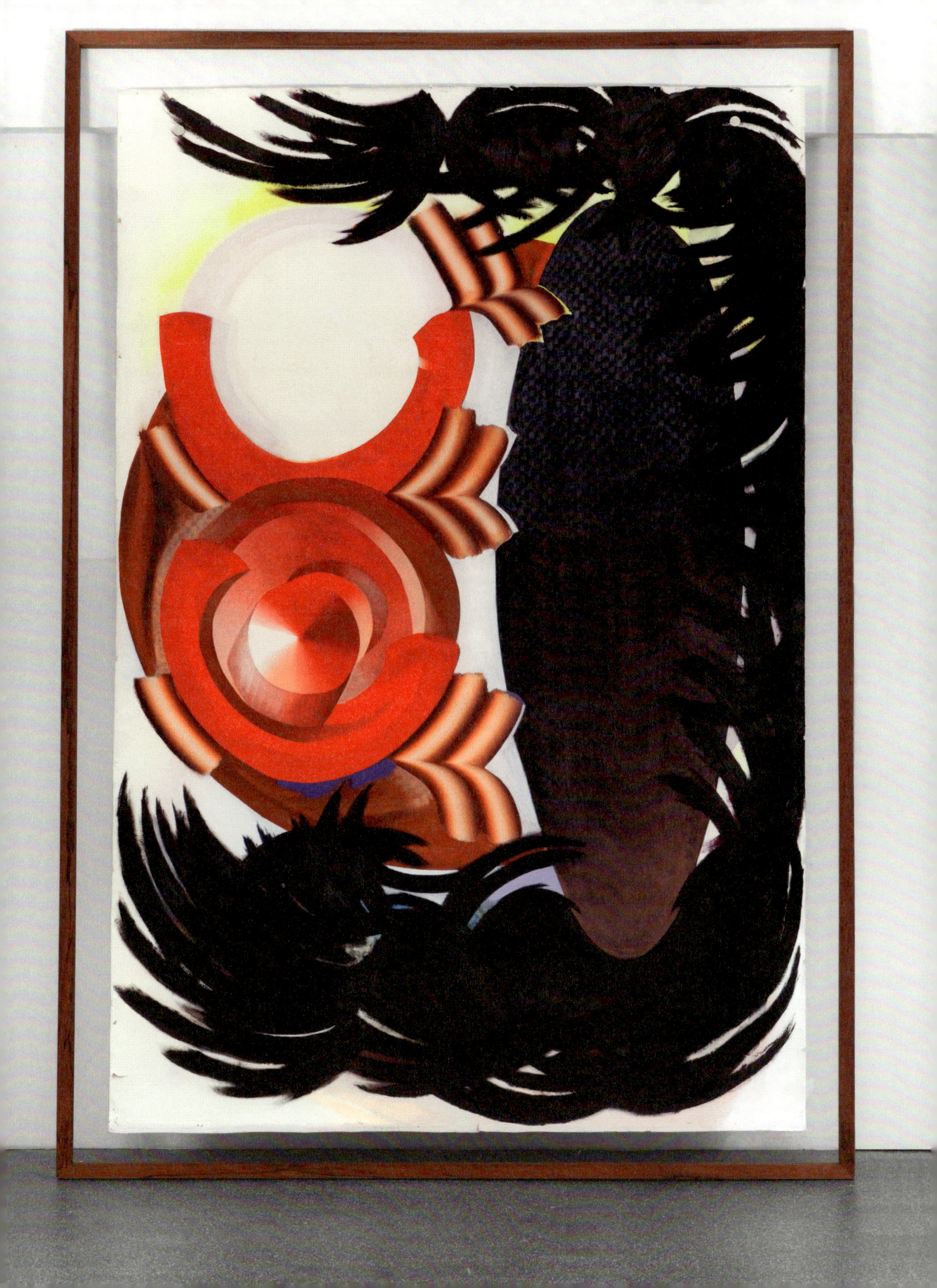

DAS INSTITUT
BUYBRÄTSCHWÖRST, 2011

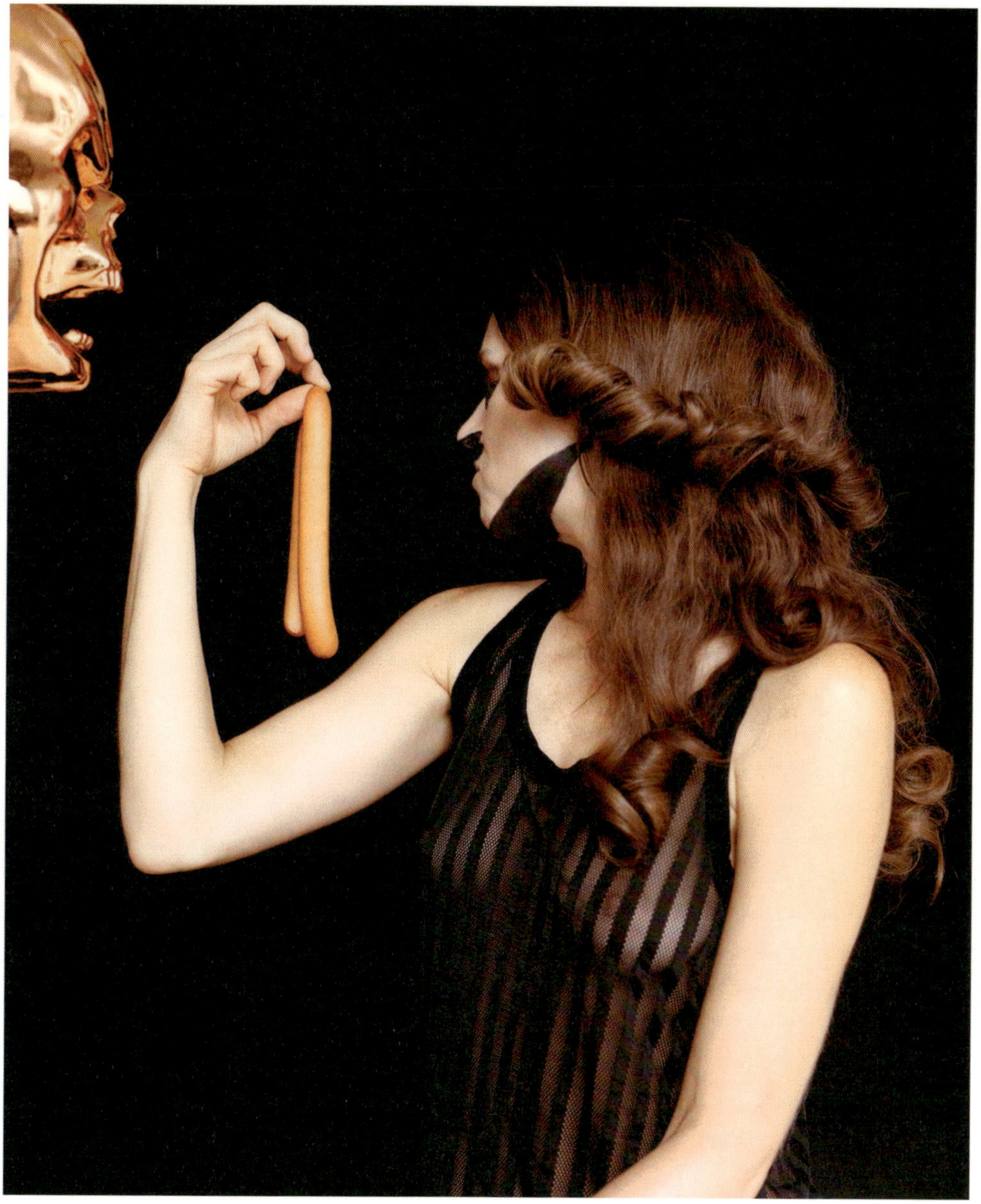

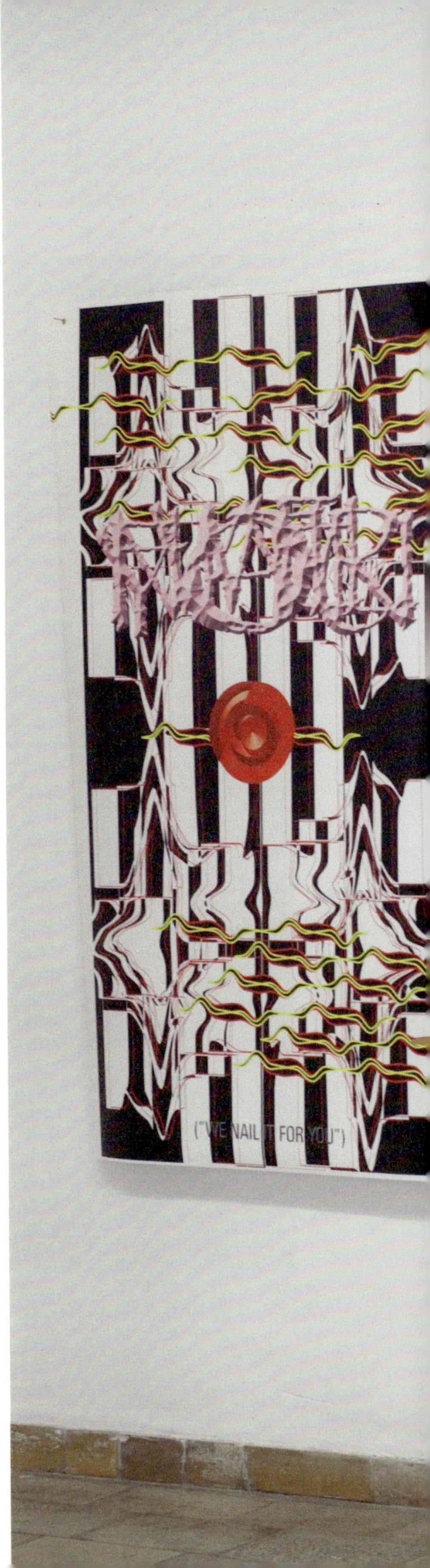

DAS INSTITUT
We Nail It for You, 2011

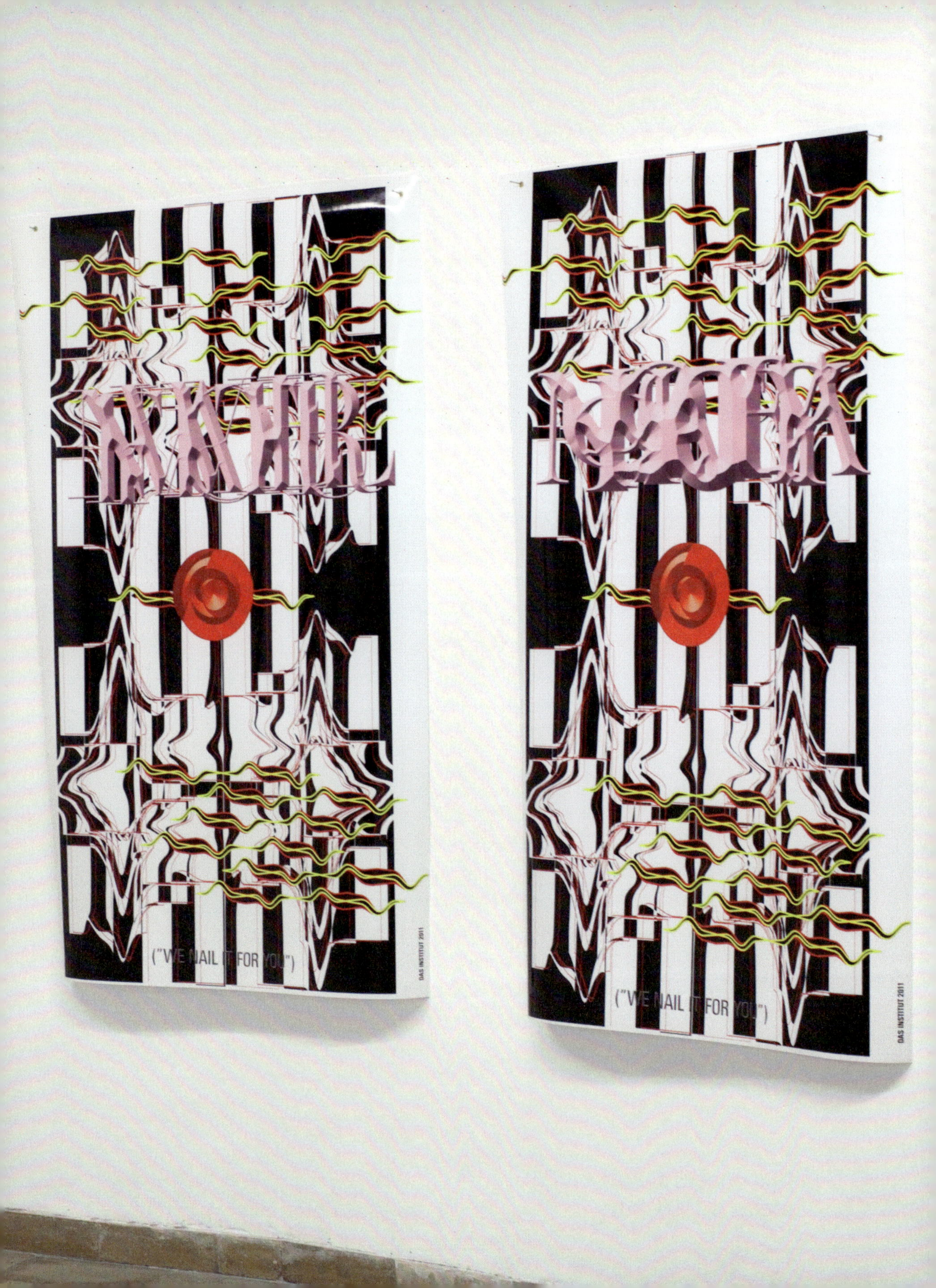
("WE NAIL IT FOR YOU")
DAS INSTITUT 2011
("WE NAIL IT FOR YOU")
DAS INSTITUT 2011

DAS INSTITUT
Nichts, Nichts, 2011

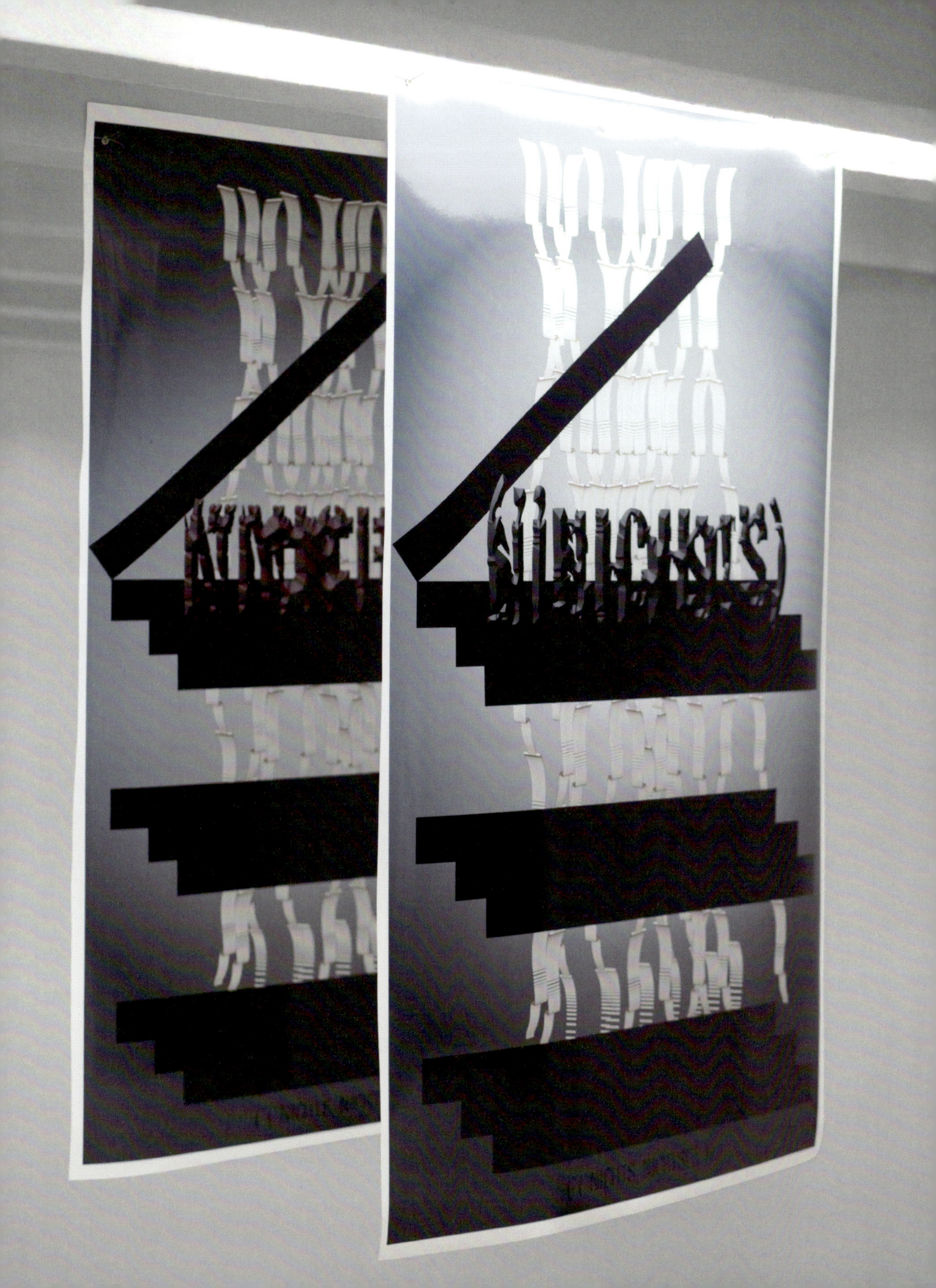

DAS INSTITUT
Di Launches Schroederline, 2011

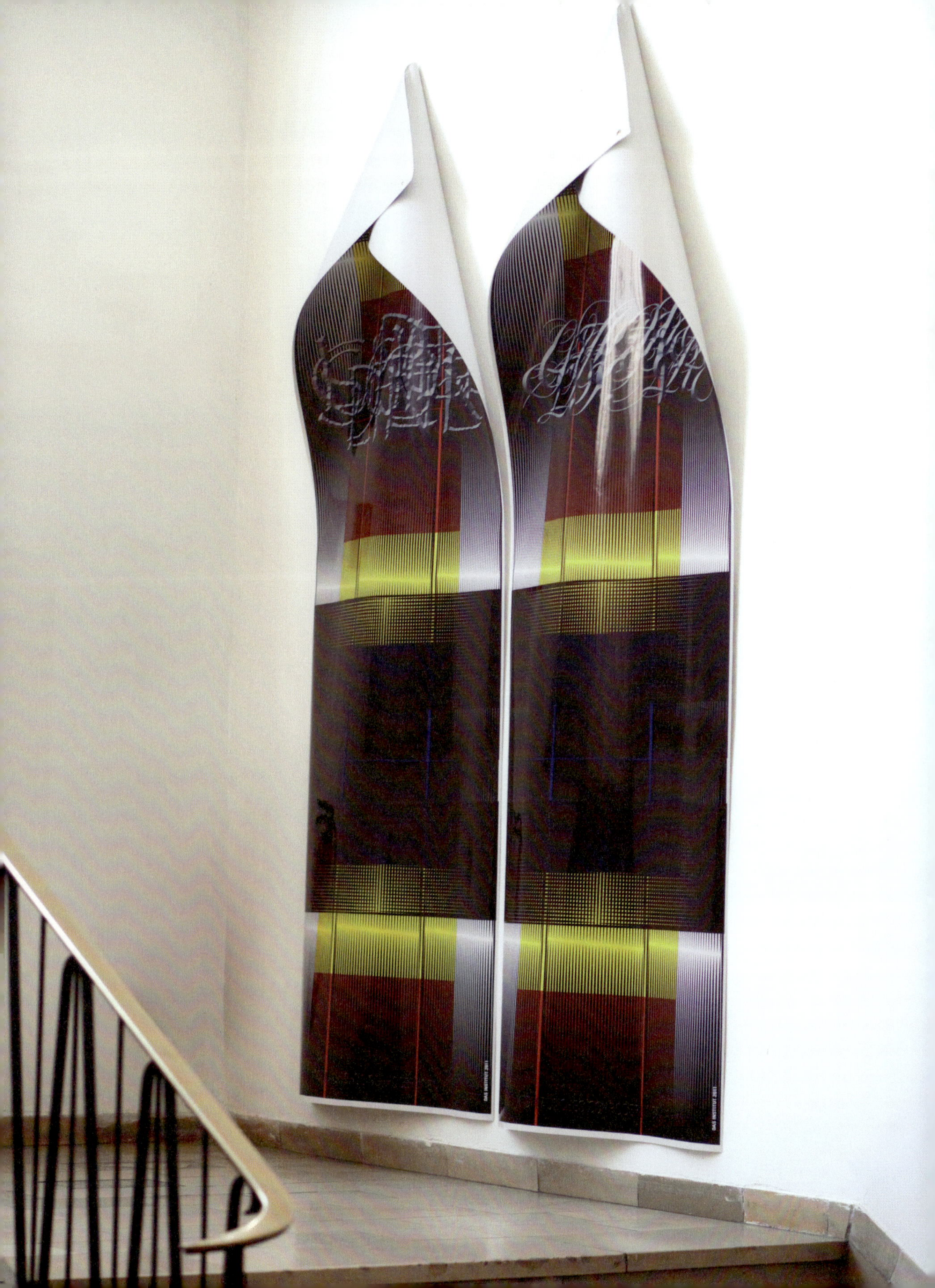
DAS INSTITUT 2011
DAS INSTITUT 2011

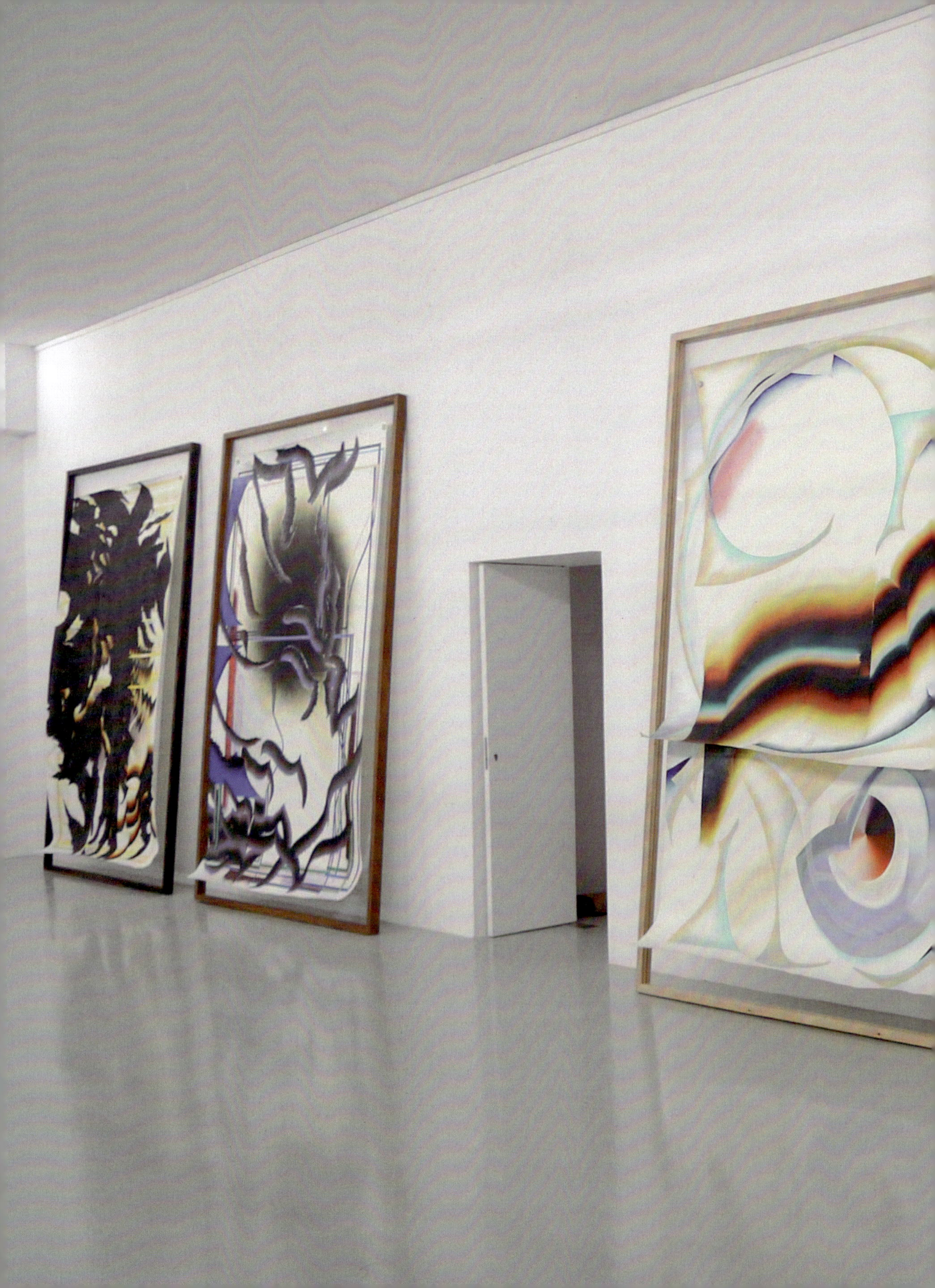

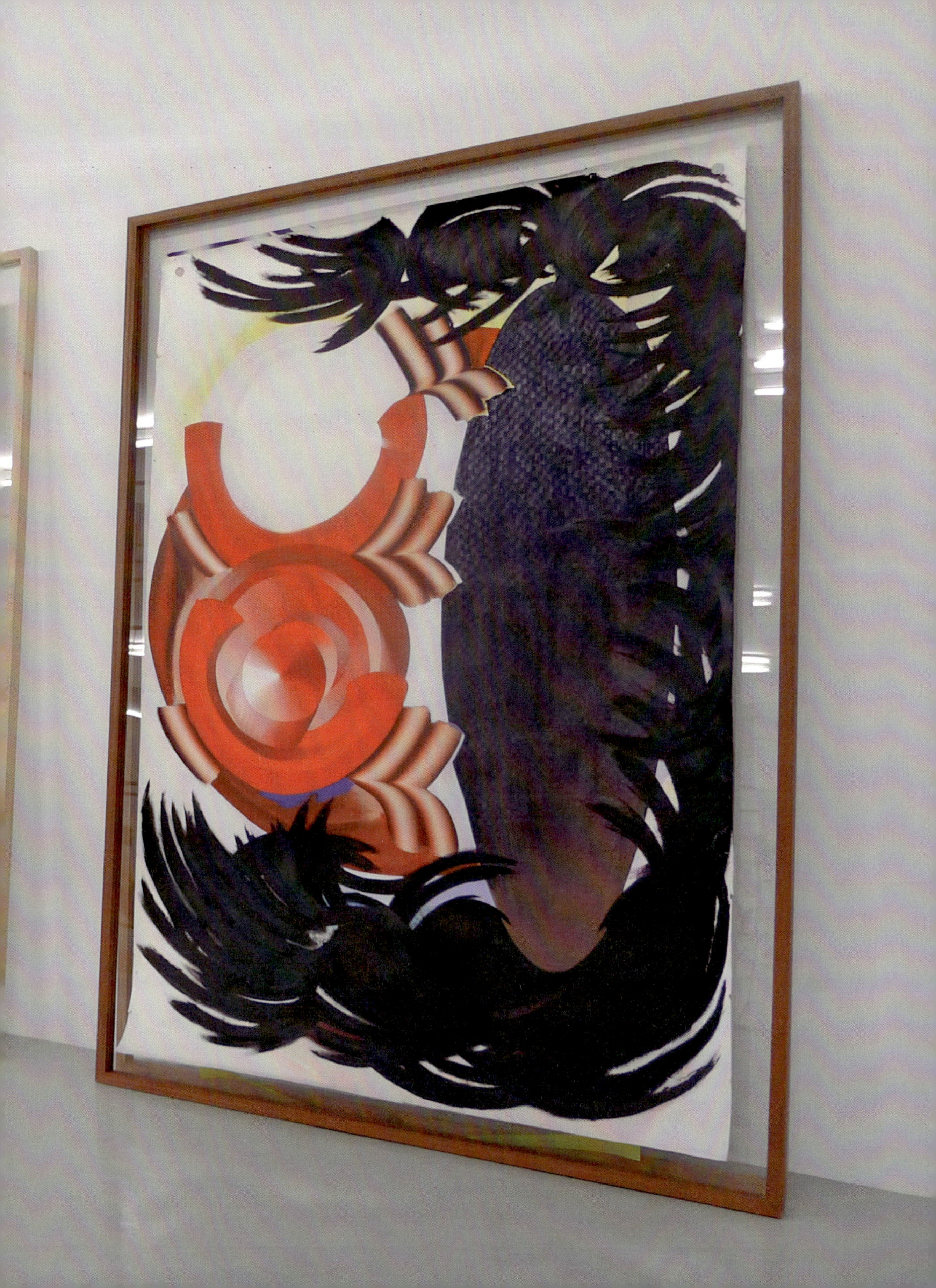

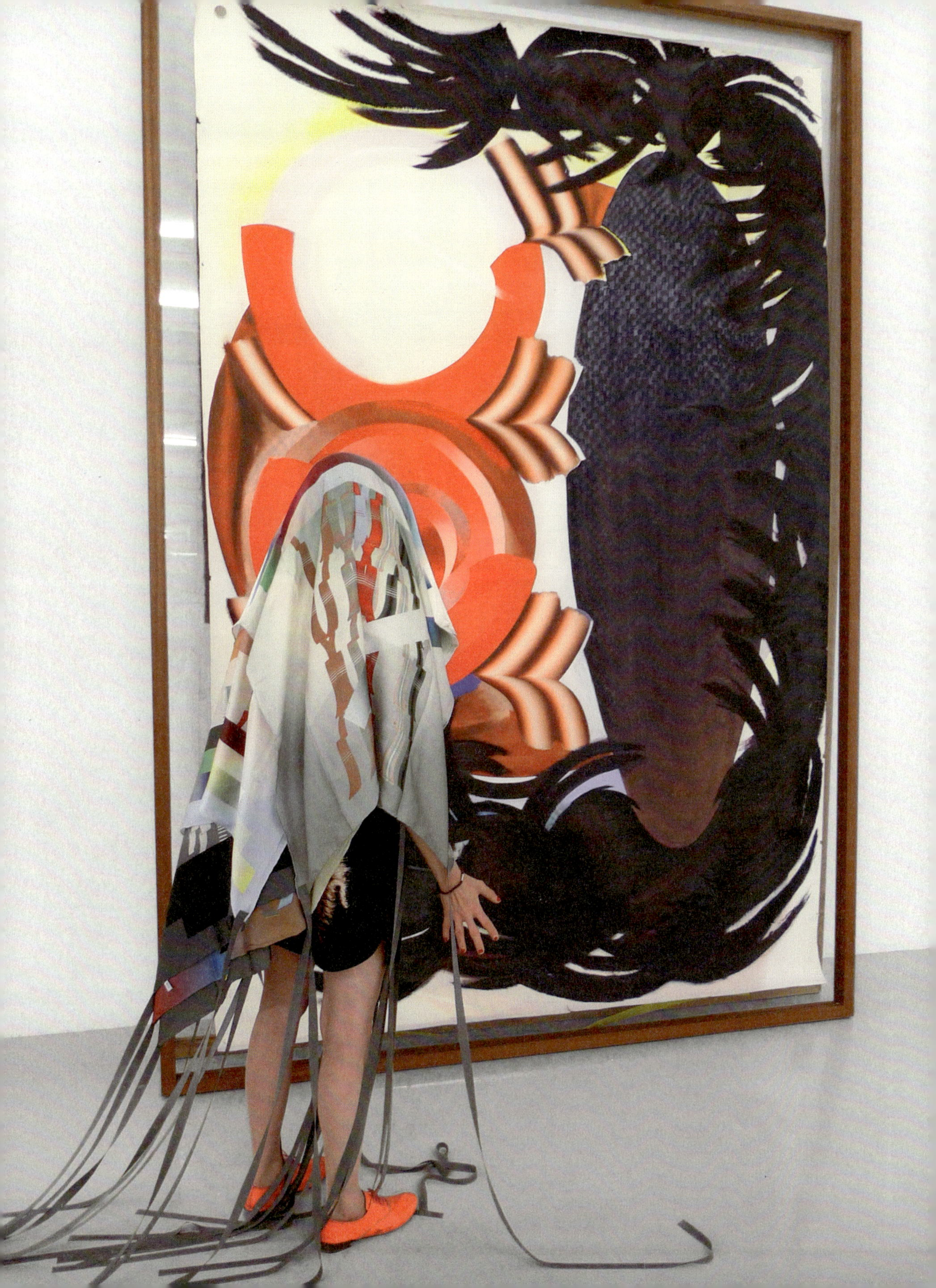

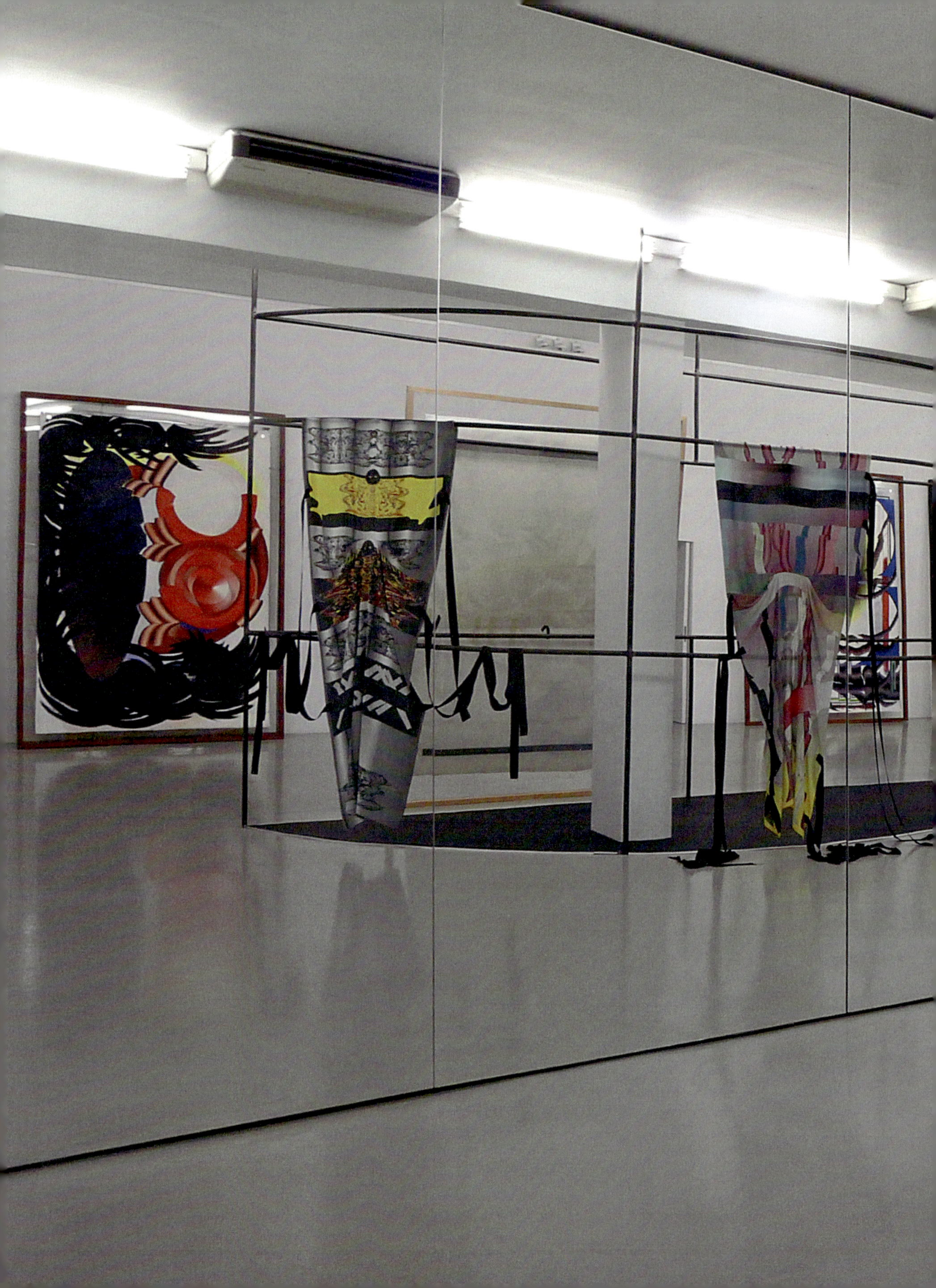

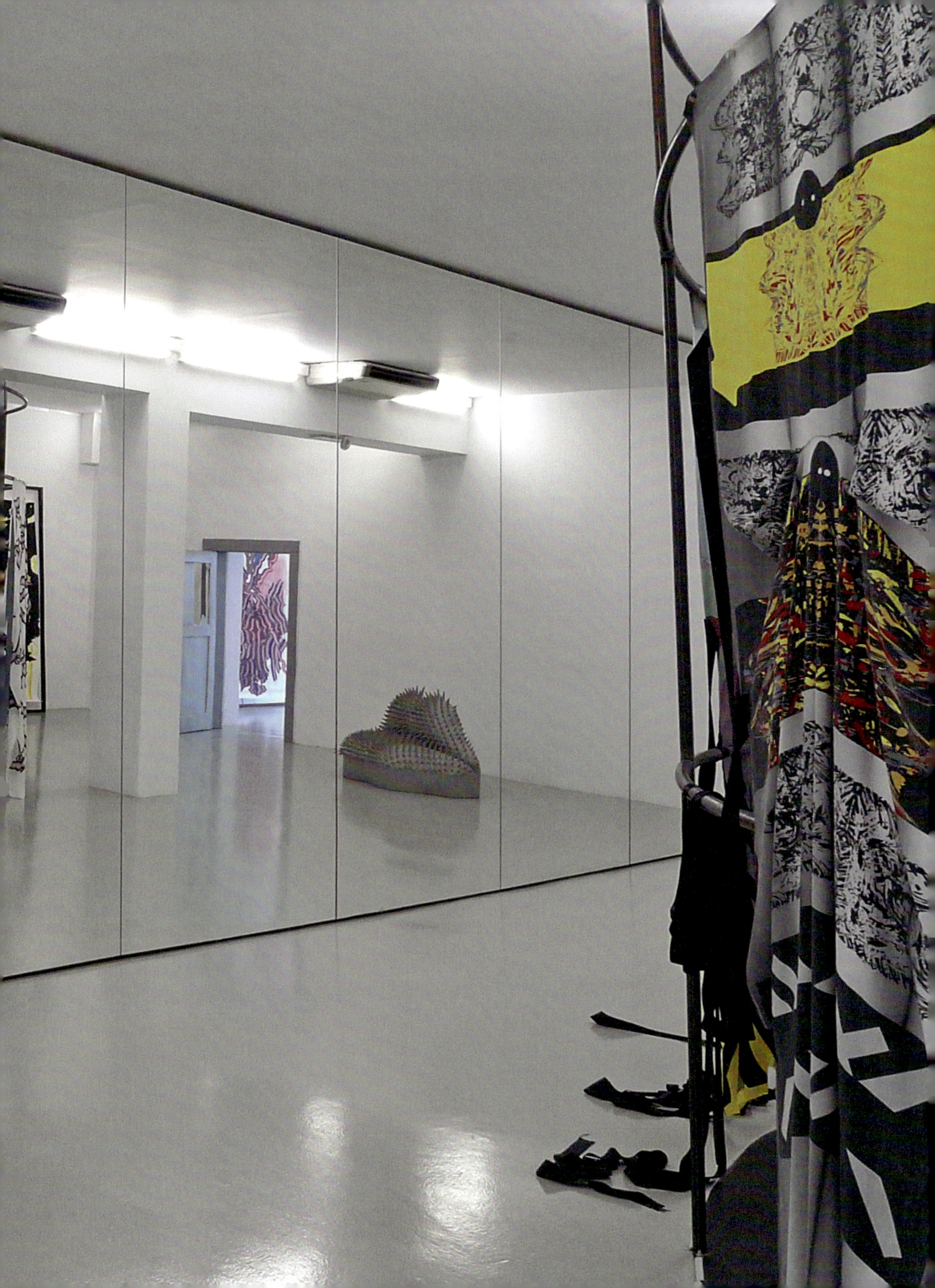

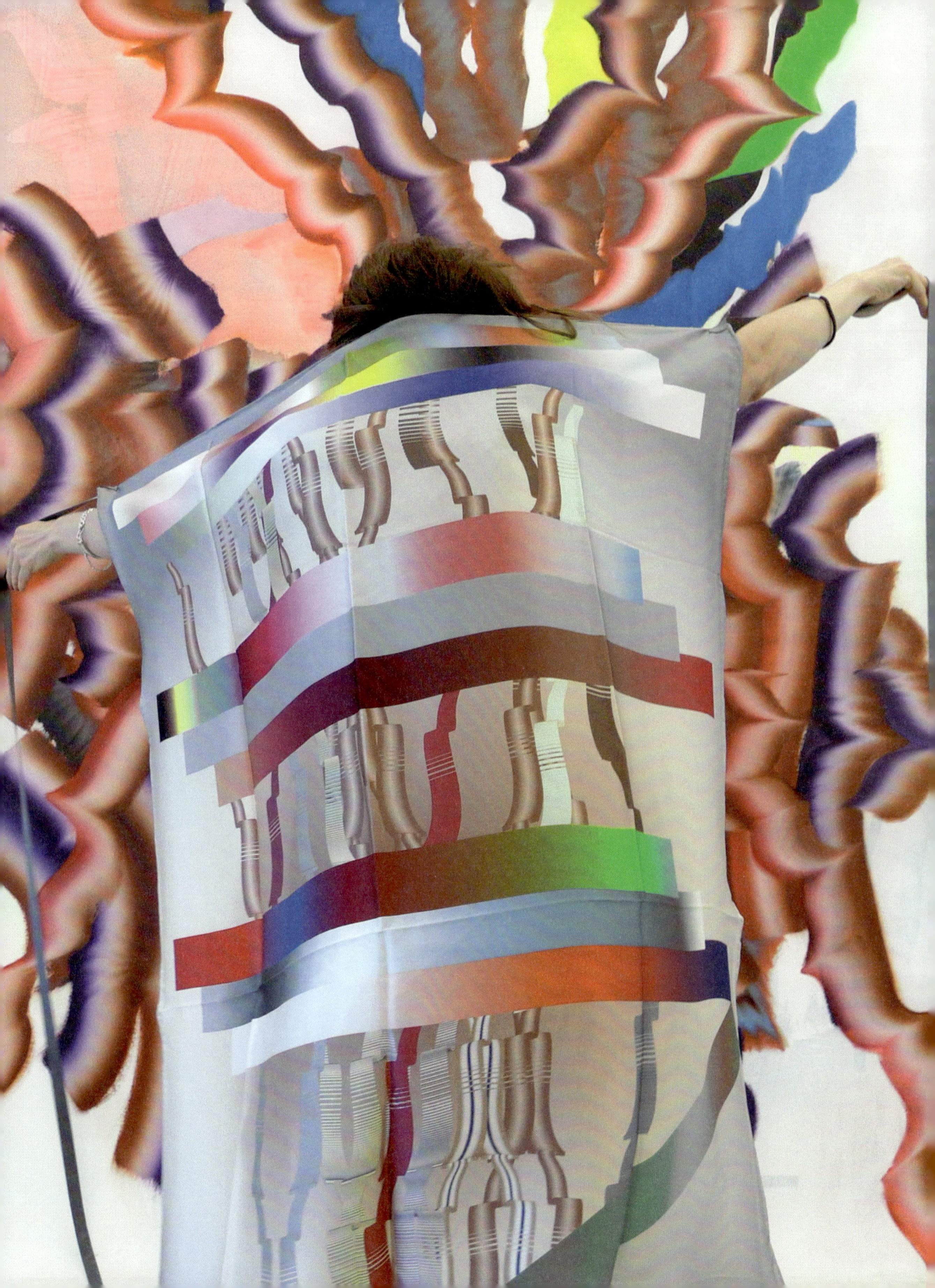

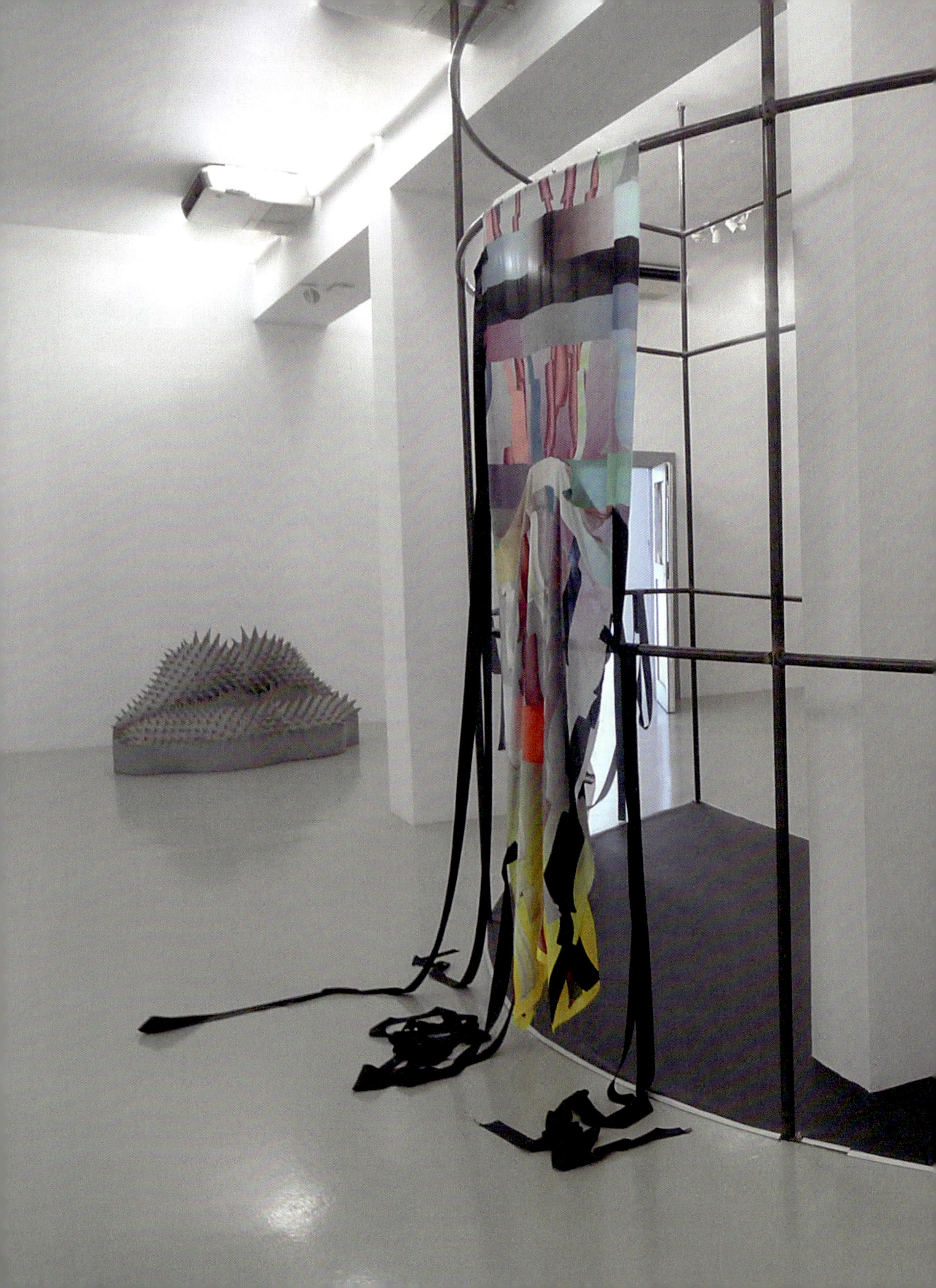

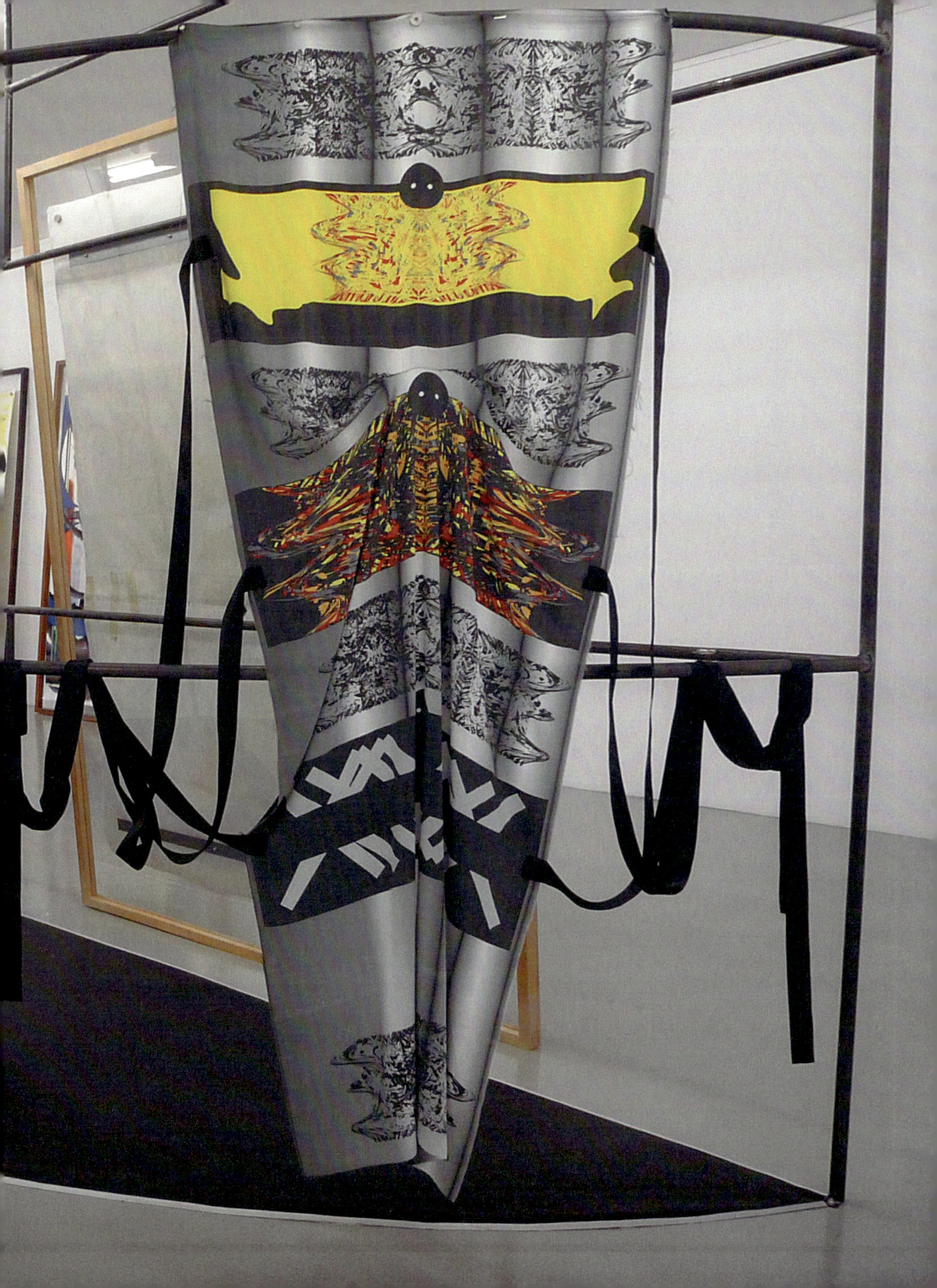

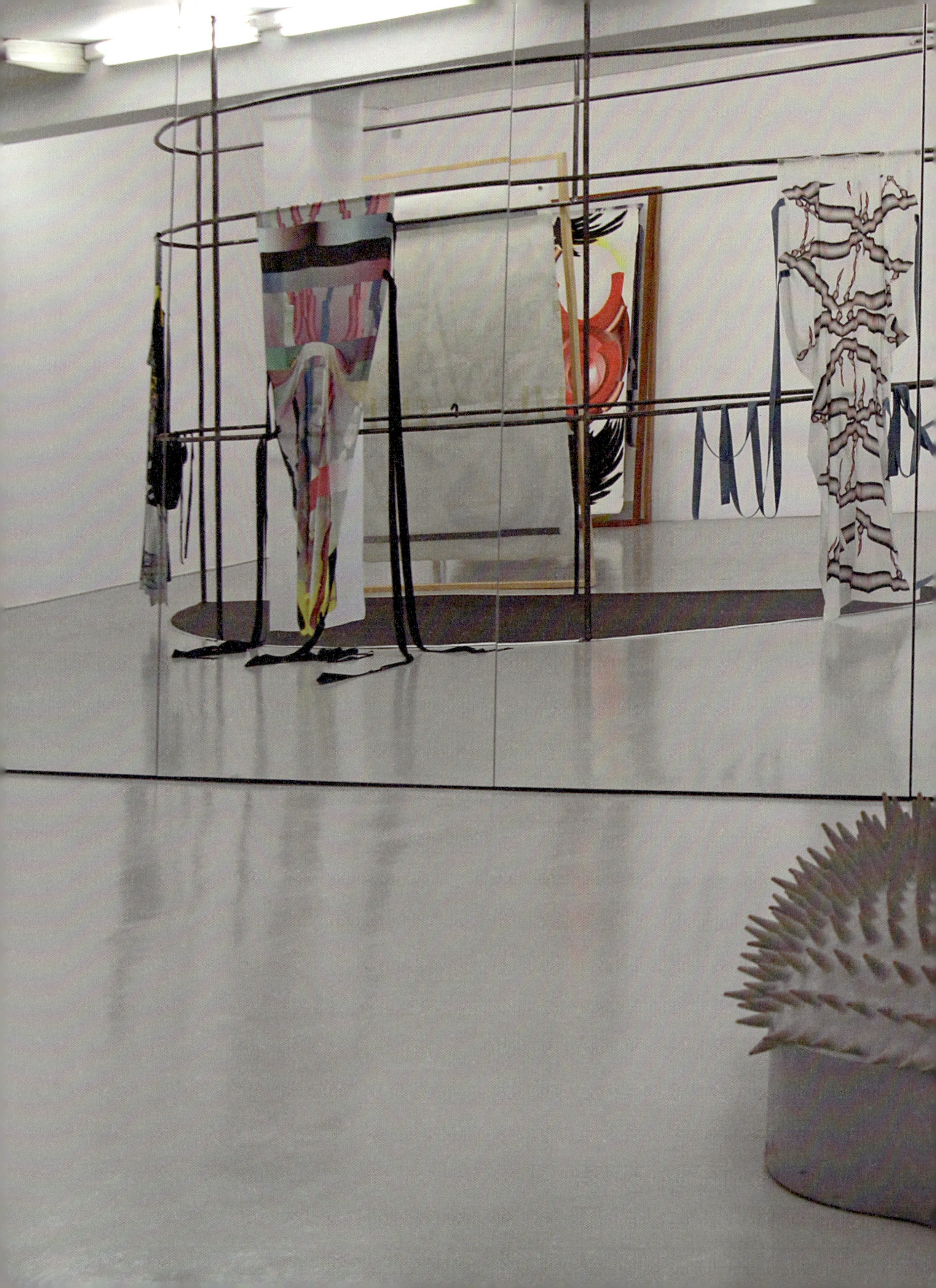

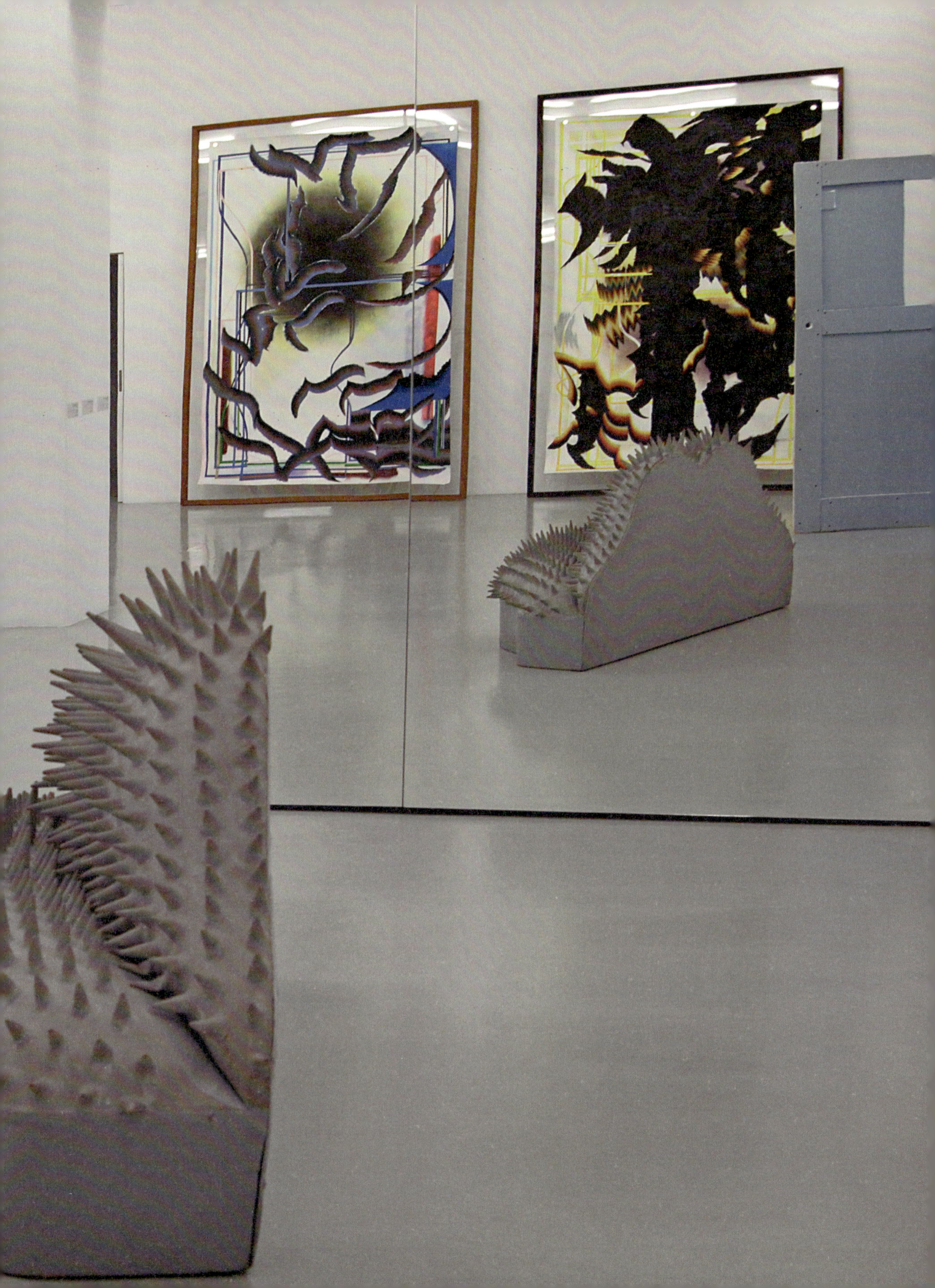

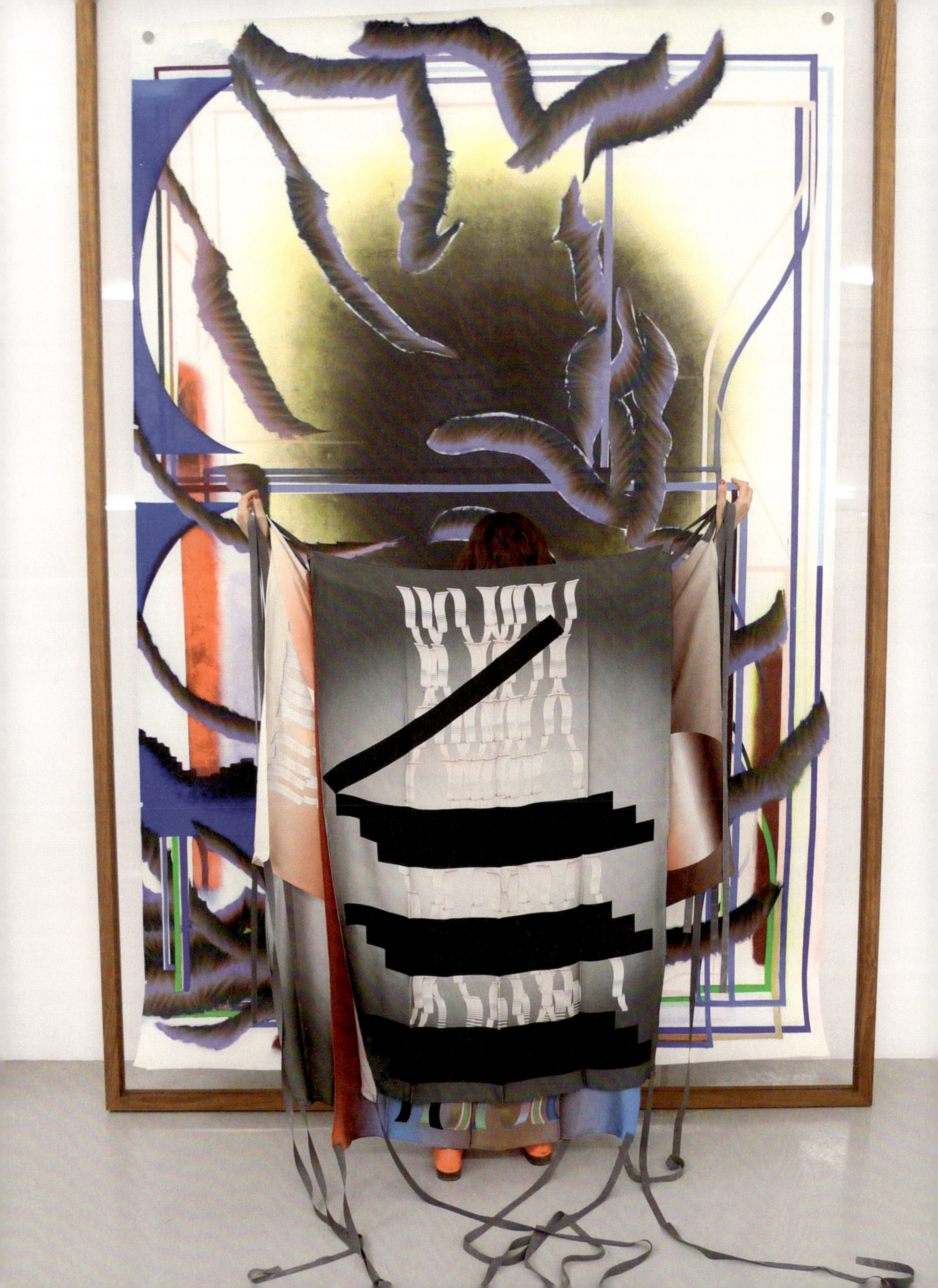

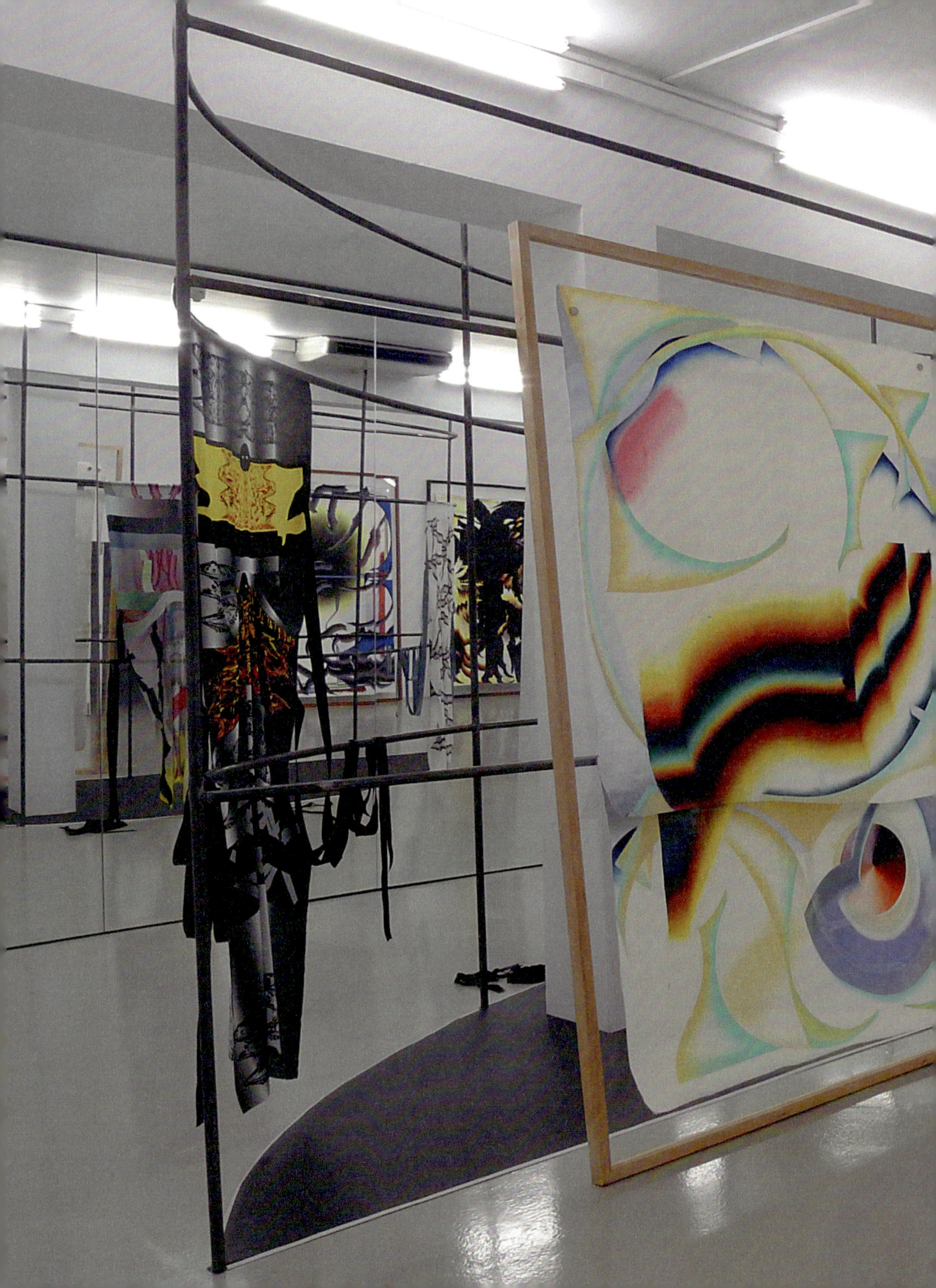

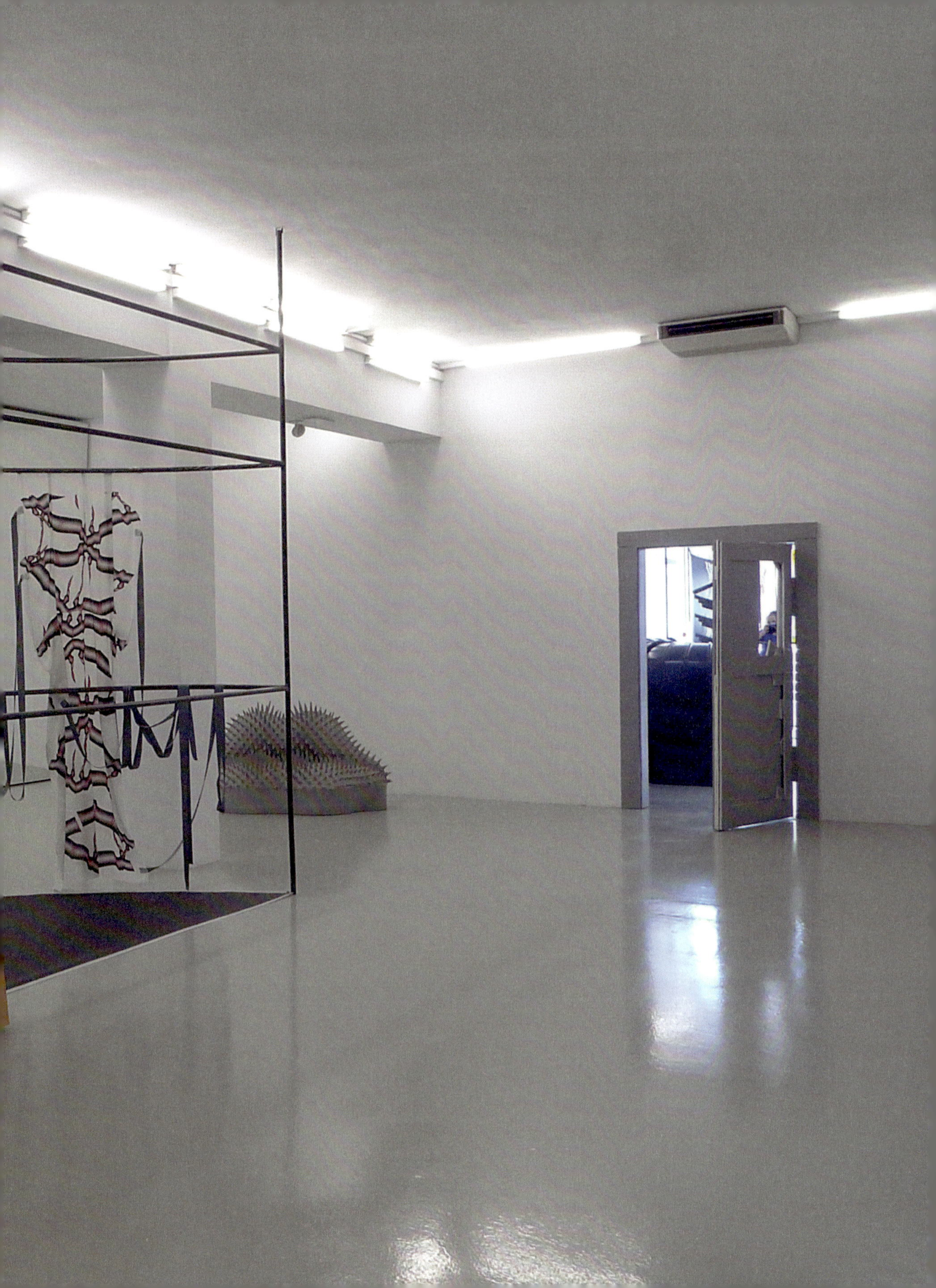

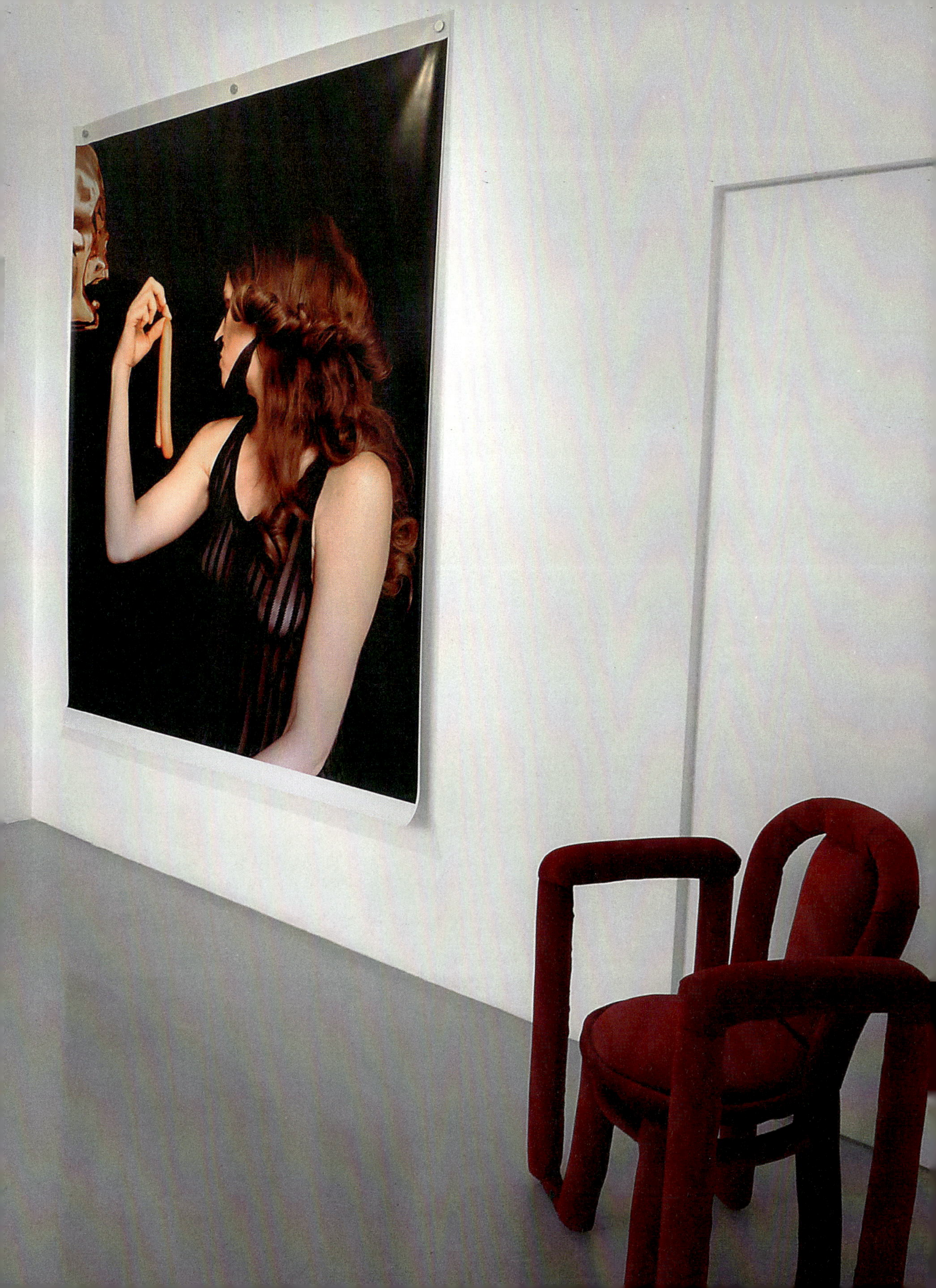

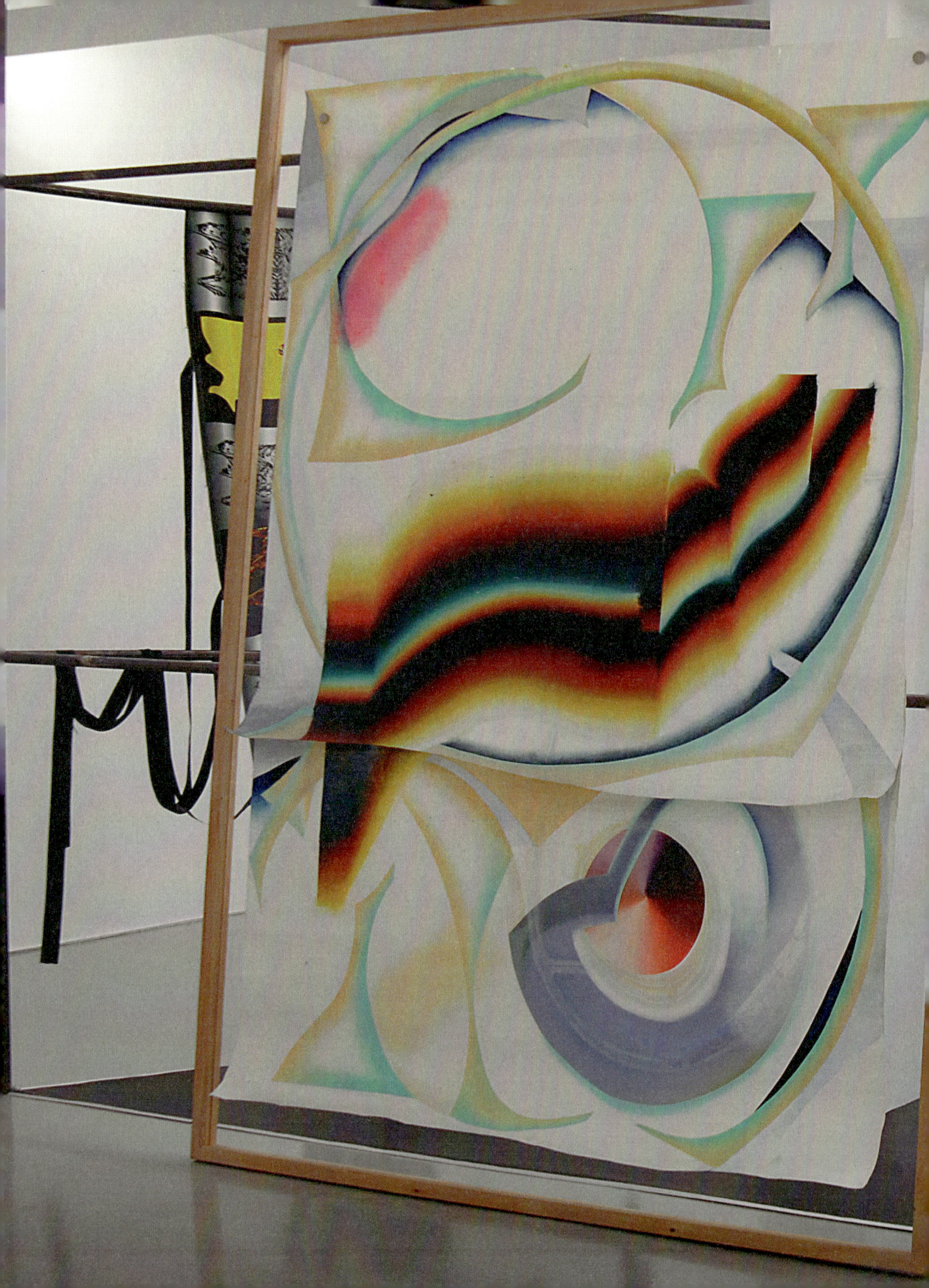

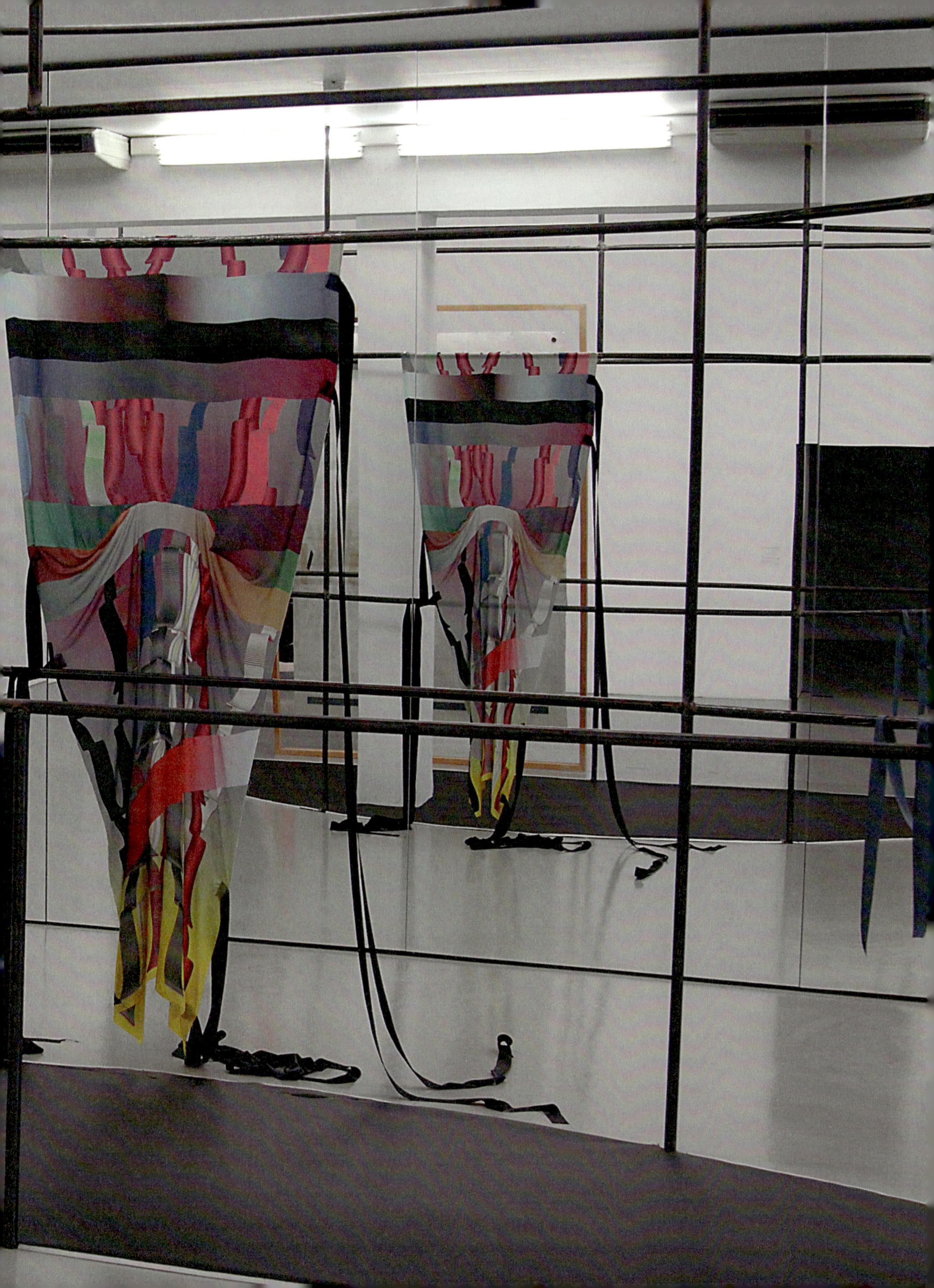

Kerstin Brätsch
Mad Madder Matter, 2013 (from the series All Ready Maid Betwixt and Between)

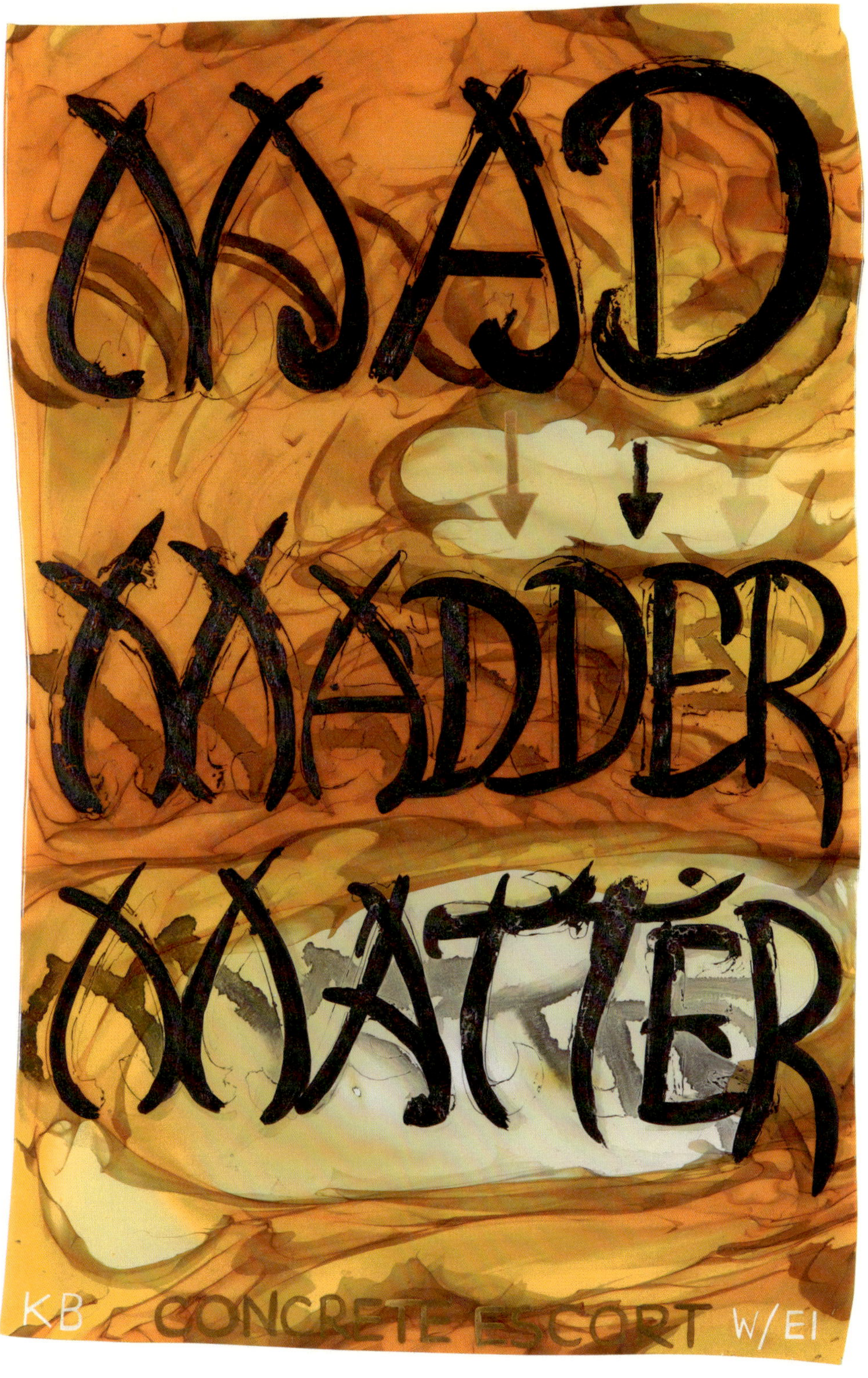
MAD
MADDER
MATTER
KB CONCRETE ESCORT W/EI

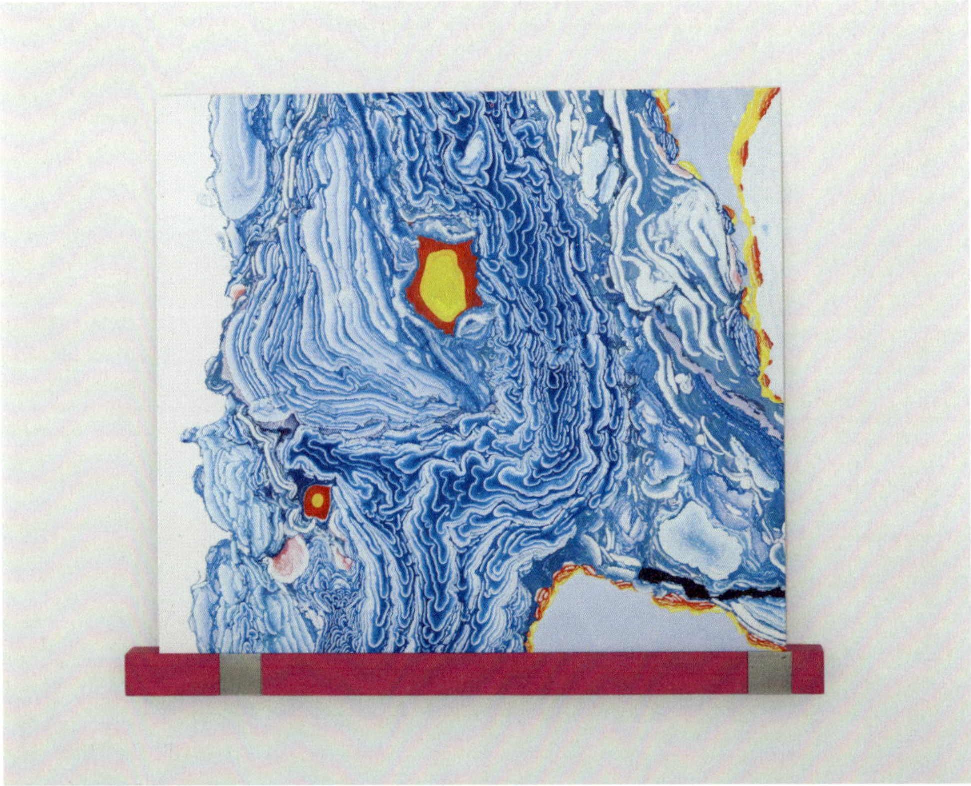

Kerstin Brätsch
Unstable Talismanic Rendering_MAP (with Gratitude to Master Marbler Dirk Lange), 2016

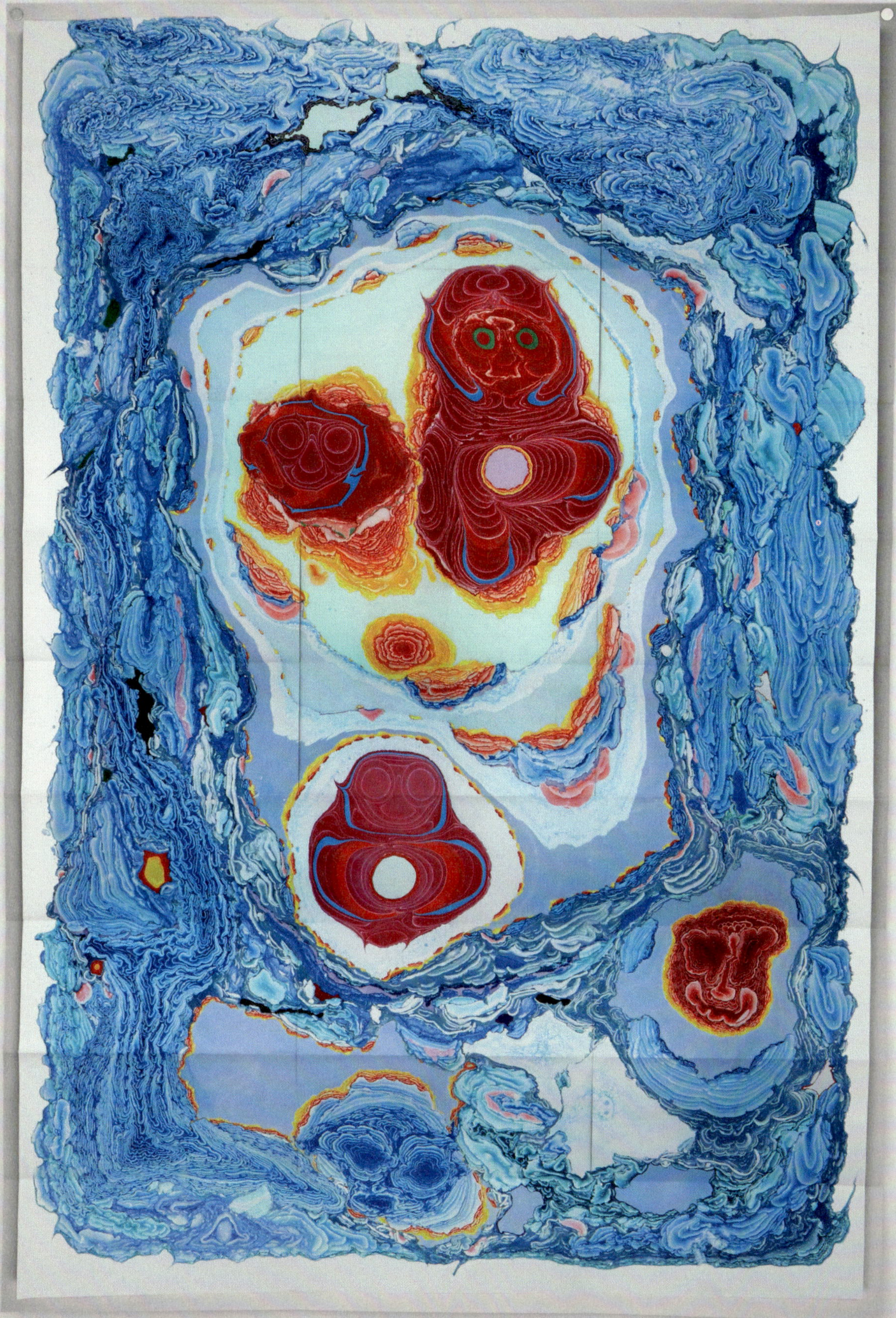

LIST OF WORKS

DAS INSTITUT
THUS! Unit 4, 2010
Two oil-on-Mylar paintings by Kerstin Brätsch for DAS INSTITUT and two digitally printed silk fabrics by Adele Röder for DAS INSTITUT
Four parts, each 381 × 122 cm (approx.)

Kerstin Brätsch for DAS INSTITUT
But Your Soul Is Too Big It Would Stick Out Everywhere, 2011
(from the series *Corporate Abstraction*)
Oil on paper, wooden frame, magnets
279.4 × 182.8 cm

Kerstin Brätsch for DAS INSTITUT
Luxus, Askese, Cocoonin, Neo Neo Biedermeier, 2011
(from the series *Corporate Abstraction*)
Oil on paper, wooden frame, magnets
279.4 × 182.8 cm

Kerstin Brätsch for DAS INSTITUT
The Random/The Violent Effect, 2011
(from the series *Corporate Abstraction*)
Oil and collage on paper, wooden frame, magnets
279.4 × 182.8 cm

Kerstin Brätsch for DAS INSTITUT
Also Known As, 2011
(from the series *Corporate Abstraction*)
Oil and collage on paper, wooden frame, magnets
279.4 × 182.8 cm

Kerstin Brätsch for DAS INSTITUT
Main Street Left, Second Right, 2011 (from the series *Corporate Abstraction*)
Oil on paper, wooden frame, magnets
279.4 × 182.8 cm

Kerstin Brätsch for DAS INSTITUT
This Is Not It, 2011 (from the series *Corporate Abstraction*)
Oil on paper, wooden frame, magnets
279.4 × 182.8 cm

DAS INSTITUT
BUYBRÄTSCHWÖRST, 2011
C-print on archival paper
240 × 182 cm

DAS INSTITUT
We Nail It for You, 2011
Digital prints on archival paper
Three parts, each 152 × 92 cm

DAS INSTITUT
Nichts, Nichts, 2011
Digital prints on archival paper
Three parts, each 152 × 92 cm

DAS INSTITUT
Di Launches Schroederline, 2011
Digital prints on archival paper
Two parts, each 269 × 91 cm

Kerstin Brätsch
Mad Madder Matter, 2013 (from the series *All Ready Maid Betwixt and Between*)
Luster on antique glass, steel bar, rubber strip
93.7 × 57.5 cm

Kerstin Brätsch
Unstable Talismanic Rendering_MAP (with Gratitude to Master Marbler Dirk Lange), 2016
Three parts:
Unique pigment print mounted on Dibond
53.4 × 58.5 cm
Hand-scored and folded pigment print
27.9 × 31.8 × 4.4 cm (unfolded 274.3 × 182.9 cm)
Unique handmade framing bar with koto wood, steel, paint, magnets
6 × 65 × 4.1 cm
Published by Lisa Ivorian-Jones for the New Museum
Edition 10/15

ARTIST BIO

Kerstin Brätsch was born in Hamburg, Germany. She received an MFA from the Universität der Künste Berlin and Columbia University, New York. Her work challenges abstraction and its aesthetic vocabulary by considering painting as a link within a system of constant production and transformation. Often in collaboration with collectives and alter egos including DAS INSTITUT (with Adele Röder), KAYA (with Debo Eilers), and UNITED BROTHERS (Ei Arakawa and Tomoo Arakawa), Brätsch addresses the merger of the means of production with the means of communication in the digital age.

Her most recent exhibitions include *Kerstin Brätsch. Innovation*, Museum Brandhorst, Munich (2017), and *Pele's Curse*, the Arts Club of Chicago (2015). As DAS INSTITUT she has exhibited at Serpentine Sackler Gallery, London (2016); Kunsthalle Zürich (2011); DESTE Foundation for Contemporary Art, Athens (2011); and Kölnischer Kunstverein, Cologne (2011), as well as in the Venice Biennale (2011). As part of KAYA she has exhibited in *Painting 2.0: Expression in the Information Age*, Museum Brandhorst, Munich (2016); *Speculations on Anonymous Materials*, Fridericianum, Kassel (2014); and in the Whitney Biennial, New York (2017). Brätsch's work has also appeared in group exhibitions such as *The Forever Now: Contemporary Painting in an Atemporal World*, the Museum of Modern Art, New York (2014–15); *The Painting Factory: Abstraction After Warhol*, the Museum of Contemporary Art, Los Angeles (2012); *Younger Than Jesus*, the New Museum, New York (2009); and the Gwangju Biennale (2010), among many others. Brätsch lives and works in New York City.

AUTHOR BIO

Massimiliano Gioni is the Edlis Neeson Artistic Director of the New Museum in New York and the artistic director of the Fondazione Nicola Trussardi in Milan. Since 2007 Gioni has curated numerous exhibitions at the New Museum, including solo shows by Paul Chan, Tacita Dean, Urs Fischer, Carsten Höller, Ragnar Kjartansson, Klara Liden, Gustav Metzger, Pipilotti Rist, Raymond Pettibon, Anri Sala, and many others, along with the group exhibitions *The Keeper* (2016), *NYC 1993: Experimental Jet Set, Trash and No Star* (2013), *Ghosts in the Machine* (2012), *Ostalgia* (2011), and *After Nature* (2008), as well as the inaugural triennial *Younger than Jesus* (2009). In Milan, with the Fondazione Nicola Trussardi, he has organized a series of exhibitions and public art projects including *Still Life* by Tacita Dean, Palazzo Dugnani (2009); Tino Sehgal, Villa Reale, Galleria d'Arte Moderna (2008); *Altri Fiori e Altre Domande* by Peter Fischli and David Weiss, Palazzo Litta (2008); *One of Many* by Paweł Althamer, Arena Civica (2007); and Maurizio Cattelan's historic *Untitled* at Piazza XXIV Maggio (2004). Gioni has curated major international exhibitions, including *The Restless Earth* at the Milan Triennial (2017), the Venice Biennale (2013), the Gwangju Biennale (2010), and the 4th Berlin Biennale (2006).

Gioni cofounded the Wrong Gallery, a traveling minigallery that initially opened in New York in 2002. He is a frequent collaborator on DESTE Foundation for Contemporary Art projects in Athens and the commissioning editor of the *2000 Words* series.

I first saw the work of Kerstin Brätsch at Basel Statements in 2011 and immediately asked her to stage an exhibition at the DESTE Foundation for Contemporary Art. I find that Kerstin's approach to painting is like no other. Using a network of references, she challenges tradition in each brushstroke, updating the medium of painting in a complex way. My sincerest gratitude must first go to Kerstin, who never ceases to surprise me. I also must thank Massimiliano Gioni for his work in commissioning all of the essays in this series and especially for writing for this volume; Karen Marta and her team at KMEC for their fastidious editorial work; and Brendan Dugan, whose innovative design has created the visual identity for the *2000 Words* series.

—Dakis Joannou

Kerstin Brätsch
2000 Words

Commissioning Editor: Massimiliano Gioni
Editor: Karen Marta
Design Concept and Cover: An Art Service
Managing Editor: Tommaso Speretta
Line Editor: Tim Gentles
Project Manager: Regina Alivisatos
Registrar: Natasha Polymeropoulos
Copy Editor: Clare Fentress
Proofreader: Lawrence Levi
Production: The Production Department

Published by:
DESTE Foundation for Contemporary Art
11 Filellinon & Em. Pappa St.
Nea Ionia 142 34
Athens, Greece
www.deste.gr

Available worldwide through:
ARTBOOK | D.A.P.
75 Broad St, Suite 630
New York, NY 10004
www.artbook.com

Available in Greece through:
The DESTE Foundation for Contemporary Art

Printed in Greece by ALTA GRAFICO S.A. Printing and Graphic Arts

ISBN: 978-618-5039-28-8

The following artworks appear in installation photographs reproduced in this volume:
Urs Fischer, *Death of a Moment*, 2007 (pages 48–49, 54–55, 58–59, 62–63)
Urs Fischer, *Untitled (Door)*, 2006 (pages 48–49, 52–53, 54–55, 58–59)
Craig Morrison, *MTV Sofa*, 1990 (pages 48–49, 52–53, 54–55, 58–59)
Chair by the Campana Brothers (page 61)

Photo credits:
Pages 21, 23, 25, 27, 29, 31, 33, 35, 38–39, 41, 43: Photos © Simon Vogel;
Page 37: Photo © Viola Yeşiltaç;
Pages 44–45, 47, 51, 57: Photos © DAS INSTITUT;
Pages 48–49, 52–55, 58–59, 61–63: Photos © Fanis Vlastaras & Rebecca Constantopoulou;
Page 65: Photo © Thomas Müller; Courtesy Kerstin Brätsch and Gavin Brown's enterprise, New York/Rome;
Pages 66, 67: Photos © Jesse Untracht-Oakner; Courtesy New Museum, New York.

Cover: Kerstin Brätsch for DAS INSTITUT, *Main Street Left, Second Right*, 2011 (from the series *Corporate Abstraction*)

Thank you to Lisa Ivorian-Jones at Ivorian-Jones Fine Art, LLC, New York; Melisa Santiago at the New Museum, New York; Marta Fontolan and Curtis Glenn at Gavin Brown's enterprise, New York/Rome; Hernán Rivera at Ponk Productions, Brooklyn